ABRAHAM LINCOLN

His Story in His Own Words

On Sunday, November 8, 1863, President Lincoln went to the photographic gallery of Alexander Gardner in Washington, D.C. He was accompanied by his secretaries, John G. Nicolay and John Hay. The President posed for several photographs, including this one. It is generally accepted as the most dramatic of the Lincoln presidential photographs. It was taken only eleven days before he delivered the Gettysburg Address.

ABRAHAM LINCOLN

His Story in His Own Words

EDITED AND WITH NOTES
BY RALPH GEOFFREY NEWMAN

"Abraham Lincoln
his hand and pen
he will be good but
God knows when."

DOUBLEDAY & COMPANY, INC.

GARDEN CITY, NEW YORK

1975

C/970 117p.

CONTENTS

Foreword	3
Kentucky Birth	7
Indiana Years	11
Sister Sarah	15
Trip to New Orleans	17
Move to Illinois	19
Black Hawk War	25
Postmaster and Surveyor	29
Illinois Legislator	31
Springfield Lawyer	33
Marriage to Mary Todd	35
The Lincoln Family	37
United States Congressman	39
The House Divided	43
Debates with Douglas	47
Nomination for President	51
Presidential Election	55
Farewell to Springfield	59
First Inaugural	63

Emancipation Proclamation   67

Commander-in-Chief   73

Gettysburg Address   77

Second Inaugural   83

Ford's Theatre   89

The Memorial   93

A Library of Essential Lincolniana   95

Reference Sources for Quotations
    Used as Chapter Headings   109

Index   113

*As a matter, wholly my own, I would
authorize no biography, without time,
and opportunity to carefully examine
and consider every word of it; . . .*

FOREWORD

In 1859, and again in 1860, Abraham Lincoln wrote short
autobiographical sketches. The first was prepared for his
friend, Jesse W. Fell, of Bloomington, Illinois, Adlai E.
Stevenson's great grandfather and one of Lincoln's earliest
supporters for the presidency. It was written in the first
person. Fell sent the sketch to Joseph J. Lewis of West
Chester, Pennsylvania, who used it in preparing an article
which was published in the *Chester County Times*,
February 11, 1860, and was then widely copied in Republican
newspapers throughout the country.

The second sketch, written in the third person, was
prepared for the guidance of John Locke Scripps, of the
Chicago Press and Tribune, who was writing a campaign
biography. Scripps's *Life of Abraham Lincoln* was published
by both the *Chicago Press and Tribune* and Horace Greeley's
New York Tribune as *Tribune Tracts No. 6.*

In this book, both of these sketches have been combined
into a single autobiographical narrative. Lincoln ended his
autobiographical writings with the campaign of 1856. The
editor has supplemented Lincoln's personal account with

3

extracts from his letters and speeches which are autobiographical in nature. To facilitate reading and to avoid confusion, the entire revised sketch is presented in the first person. Except for change of pronouns and the insertion of a few words to serve as a "bridge" between the various segments, no other liberties have been taken with Lincoln's text. Where Lincoln writings were not available to cover certain important periods in his life, the editor has supplied his own comments, which are readily distinguishable from Lincoln's own text.

ABRAHAM LINCOLN
His Story in His Own Words

What Kentuckian, worthy of his place,
would not do this? Gentlemen, I too,
am a Kentuckian.

KENTUCKY BIRTH

I was born February 12, 1809, in Hardin, now in the more recently formed county of Larue, Kentucky. My parents were both born in Virginia, of undistinguished families —second families, perhaps I should say. My father, Thomas, and grandfather, Abraham, were born in Rockingham county, Virginia, whither their ancestors had come from Berks County, Pennsylvania. My lineage has been traced no farther back than this. The family were originally Quakers, though in later times they have fallen away from the peculiar habits of that people. An effort to identify them with the New England family of the same name ended in nothing more definite, than a similarity of Christian names in both families, such as Enoch, Levi, Mordecai, Solomon, Abraham, and the like. Grandfather Abraham had four brothers—Isaac, Jacob, John and Thomas. So far as known, the descendants of Jacob and John are still in Virginia. Isaac went to a place where Virginia, North Carolina, and Tennessee join; and his descendants are in that region. Thomas came to Kentucky, and after many years, died there, whence his descendants went to Missouri. My paternal grandfather, Abraham Lincoln, emigrated from Virginia, to Kentucky, about 1781 or 2, where a year or two later, he was killed by Indians, not in battle, but by stealth, when he was laboring to open a farm in the forest. He left a widow, three sons and two daughters. The eldest son, Mordecai, remained in Kentucky till late in life, when he removed to Hancock county, Illinois, where soon after he died, and where several of his descendants still reside. The second son, Josiah, removed at an early day to a place on Blue River, now within Hancock county, Indiana; but no recent information of him, or his family, has been obtained. The eldest sister, Mary, married Ralph Crume and some of her descendants are now known to be in Breckenridge county, Kentucky. The second sister, Nancy, married William Brumfield, and her family are not known to have left Kentucky, but there is no recent information from them. My father, at the death of his father, was but six years of age; and because of the very narrow circumstance of his mother, even in childhood was a wandering laboring boy; and he grew up literally without education. He never did more in the way of writing than to bunglingly sign his own name. Before he was grown, he passed one year as a hired hand with his uncle Isaac on Watauga, a branch of the Holston river. Getting back into Kentucky, and having reached his 28th year, he married Nancy Hanks—mother of the present subject—in the year 1806. She was also born in Virginia; and relatives of hers of the name of Hanks, and of other names, now reside in Coles, in Macon, and in Adams counties, Illinois, and also in Iowa. I have no brother or sister of the whole or half blood. I had a sister, older than myself, who was grown and married, but died many years ago, leaving no child. Also a brother, younger than me, who died in infancy.

He was born in a one-room log cabin three miles south of Hodgenville, and about fourteen miles from Elizabethtown, on the Big South fork of Nolin Creek. Thomas Jefferson was completing his second term as President; Napoleon Bonaparte dominated Europe. His sister, Sarah, two years older, and his mother's cousin, Dennis Hanks, ten years his senior, were among his childhood companions. Two years after Abe's birth, Thomas Lincoln moved his family to a new cabin on Knob Creek, fifteen miles northeast of Nolin Creek, and here he started school.

Before leaving Kentucky my sister and I were sent for short periods, to A.B.C. schools, the first kept by Zachariah Riney, and the second by Caleb Hazel. At this time my father resided on Knob Creek, on the road from Bardstown, Kentucky to Nashville, Tennessee at a point three, or three and a half miles south or southwest of Atherton's ferry on the Rolling Fork.

It was here at the Knob Creek farm that his younger brother, Thomas, was born and died in infancy, in 1811. Little Abraham soon learned to follow his father in the fields, and was put to work at simple tasks—dropping seeds, picking berries and later carrying water and bringing tools. Thomas Lincoln soon found himself involved in difficulties regarding the title to his farm, and by 1816 had grown discouraged and decided to move to a new state.

I am happy to meet you on this occasion,
and enter again the state of my early
life, and almost of maturity.

INDIANA YEARS

We removed from Kentucky to what is now Spencer county, Indiana, in my eighth year. This removal was partly on account of slavery; but chiefly on account of the difficulty in land titles in Kentucky. We reached our new home about the time the State came into the Union. It was a wild region, with many bears and other wild animals still in the woods. We settled in an unbroken forest; and the clearing away of surplus wood was the great task ahead. Though very young, I was large for my age, and had an axe put into my hands at once; and from that till within my twenty-third year, I was almost constantly handling that most useful instrument—less, of course, in plowing and harvesting seasons. At this place I took an early start as a hunter, which was never much improved afterwards. (A few days before the completion of my eighth year, in the absence of my father, a flock of wild turkeys approached the new log cabin, and I with a rifle gun, standing inside, shot through a crack, and killed one of them. I have never since pulled a trigger on any larger game.)

The new Lincoln homesite was located in what is now Spencer County, at Pigeon Creek. The first winter in the community was grim—the family subsisted on game and little else. Water had to be carried almost a mile. The family survived, and a year later, October 15, 1817, Thomas Lincoln made a preliminary payment of sixteen dollars, and made a commitment to pay a total of three hundred and twenty dollars for his 160 acres. In the summer of 1818 an epidemic of the "milk-sick" swept through southern Indiana. It was probably caused by cattle absorbing poison from certain plants and roots and passing the lethal effect on in their milk. The sorrow and pain of death came to the little Lincoln cabin.

In the autumn of 1818 my mother died; and a year afterwards my father married Mrs. Sally Johnston, at Elizabethtown, Kentucky—a widow, with three children of her first marriage. She proved a good and kind mother to me and is still living [1860] in Coles county, Illinois. There were no children of the second marriage. My father's residence continued at the same place in Indiana, till 1830. There I grew up. There were some schools, so called; but no qualification was ever required of a teacher, beyond *"readin, writin, and cipherin,"* to the Rule of Three. If a straggler supposed to understand Latin, happened to sojourn in the neighborhood, he was looked upon as a wizard. There was absolutely nothing to excite ambition for education. Of course when I came of age I did not know much. Still somehow, I could read, write, and cipher to the Rule of Three; but that was all. I have not been to school since. The little advance I now have upon this store of education, I have picked up from time to time under the pressure of necessity. While in Indiana, I went to A.B.C. schools by littles, kept successively by Andrew Crawford, James Swaney, and Azel W. Dorsey. I do not remember any other. The family of Mr. Dorsey now resides in Schuyler county, Illinois. I now think that the aggregate of all my schooling did not amount to one year. I was never in a college or academy as a student; and never inside of a college or academy building till since I had a law license. After I had separated from my father, I studied English grammar, imperfectly of course, but so as to speak and write as well as I now do. I studied and nearly mastered the six books of Euclid, since I was a member of Congress. I regret my want of education, and do what I can to supply the want. In my tenth year I was kicked by a horse, and apparently killed for a time.

*I was not born at Elizabethtown; but my
mother's first child, a daughter, two
years older than myself, and now long
deceased, . . .*

SISTER SARAH

As a school boy young Abe had scribbled some rhymes in his
sum book sheets. He would continue to write poetry long
after his school days were over.

> Abraham Lincoln is my name
> And with my pen I wrote the same
> I wrote in both hast and speed
> and left it here for fools to read.

> Abraham Lincoln his hand and pen
> he will be good but God knows when

In 1826, his sister Sarah married Aaron Grigsby, a young
man from the Pigeon Creek community. She and the young
farmer set up their own household, but tragedy was to strike
this marriage in a short time. On January 20, 1828, Sarah
Lincoln Grigsby, aged twenty-one, died in childbirth and was
buried in the graveyard of the Pigeon Creek Church.

Lincoln had never liked the members of the Grigsby
family, and it is believed by some that he held her husband
responsible for his sister's death. In any event, a sort of feud

developed between Abraham Lincoln and the Grigsby clan.
When, in the spring of 1828, two of the Grigsby brothers,
Reuben and Charles, married sisters in a joint wedding
ceremony, it was claimed that young Lincoln was the prime
mover in a practical joke which resulted in the brides being
sent, temporarily, to the wrong beds on their wedding night.
Though the mistake was corrected and no harm was done, it
did result in a very embarrassing situation. Lincoln himself
made the incident known through some bawdy verses written
in a Biblical style, with the title, "The Chronicles of Reuben."
Almost twenty years later, he would recall his youth in
Indiana in a poem written after he had revisited the State.

> My childhood's home I see again,
>   and sadden with the view;
> And still, as memory crowds my brain,
>   There's pleasure in it too.
>
> Near twenty years have passed away
>   Since here I bid farewell
> To woods and fields, and scenes of play,
>   And playmates loved so well.
>
> I hear the loved survivors tell
>   How nought from death could save,
> Till every sound appears a knell,
>   And every spot a grave.
>
> I range the fields with pensive tread,
>   And pace the hollow rooms,
> And feel (companions of the dead)
>   I'm living in the tombs.

The final stroke in opening the Mississippi never should, and I think never will, be forgotten.

TRIP TO NEW ORLEANS

It was in the same year, 1828, that James Gentry, a merchant of nearby Gentryville, hired Lincoln to aid his son, Allen, in taking a cargo, by flatboat, down the Ohio and Mississippi rivers. This adventure took him to New Orleans, the first really large city he had ever seen. He was introduced to urban life and had a closer view of that "Peculiar Institution," slavery.

When I was nineteen, still residing in Indiana, I made my first trip upon a flatboat to New Orleans. I was a hired hand merely; and I and a son of the owner, without other assistance, made the trip. The nature of part of the cargoload, as it was called—made it necessary for us to linger along the Sugar coast—and one night we were attacked with intent to kill and rob us. We were hurt some in the melee, but succeeded in driving the attackers from the boat, and then "cut cable," "weighed anchor" and left.

New Orleans was a picturesque place, a city with a foreign flavor, teeming with the multitudes who had come down the river in flatboats, mingling with crews of ocean-going vessels, local merchants and visiting businessmen. They all combined to make this Louisiana metropolis a market place where a variety of languages, frontier slang, English, Spanish and French could be heard. Gamblers, drunkards, prostitutes and speculators all added to the flavor of the most exciting city in the United States. It was a new experience for Abraham Lincoln.

I must care for the whole nation; but I hope it will be no injustice to any other state, for me to indulge a little home pride, that Illinois does not disappoint us.

MOVE TO ILLINOIS

Some of the members of the Hanks family had moved to Illinois, and Thomas Lincoln, back in Indiana, was intrigued by the glowing reports of the new country which came from John Hanks and others who had settled in Macon county. The death of Sarah and rumors of another wave of the "milk-sick" were sufficient to persuade him to contemplate a move to another state. By 1827, he had completed payment on a portion of the Pigeon Creek farm. He sold this land to Charles Grigsby for $125.00, gathered his family and all of their possessions, livestock, wagons and supplies, and moved west.

At twenty-one, March 1st, 1830—I came to Illinois. My father and family, with the families of two daughters and sons-in-law, of my stepmother, left the old homestead in Indiana, and came to Illinois. The mode of conveyance was wagons drawn by ox-teams. I drove one of the teams. We reached the county of Macon, and stopped there some time within the same month of March. My father and family settled a new place on the north side of the

Sangamon river, at the junction of the timberland and prairie, about ten miles westerly from Decatur. Here we built a log-cabin, into which we removed, and made sufficient rails to fence ten acres of ground, fenced and broke the ground, and raised a crop of sown corn upon it the same year. These are, or supposed to be, the rails about which so much is being said just now, though they are far from being the first, or only rails ever made by me.

The sons-in-law were temporarily settled at other places in the county. In the autumn all hands were greatly afflicted with ague and fever, to which we had not been used, and by which we were greatly discouraged—so much that we determined on leaving the county. We remained, however, through the succeeding winter, which was the winter of the very celebrated "deep snow" of Illinois.

It was here, in Macon County, that Lincoln signed (as far as it is known), his first political document. On May 26, 1830, he, along with John D. Johnston, his step-brother John Hanks, and others, signed a petition endorsed "to change the present place of holding Elections in said Precinct from Permenius Smallwoods to the Court House in Decatur." During the political campaign that followed, he delivered his first political speech. W. L. W. Ewing and John F. Posey were seeking election to the state legislature. When the two men came to Decatur, Lincoln was persuaded to speak in their behalf. It was said that he made the best speech of the day. At the August election, both Ewing and Posey were elected.

In February, 1831, a visitor from Hickman Creek, Kentucky, came to Macon County. A short, enterprising, shrewd individual, this trader and speculator set off a chain of events which were to completely change Lincoln's life. Denton Offutt wanted John Hanks to pilot a flatboat, filled with provisions for sale, to New Orleans as soon as weather conditions would permit. Hanks introduced Lincoln and John D. Johnston to Offutt, and as a result Abe traveled to the southern city a second time.

During that winter, I, together with my step-mother's son, John D. Johnston, and John Hanks, yet residing in Macon county, hired ourselves to one Denton Offutt, to take a flatboat from Beardstown, Illinois to New Orleans; and for that purpose, were to join him—Offutt—at Springfield, Illinois so soon as the snow should go off. When it did go off which was about the 1st of March 1831—the county was so flooded, as to make traveling by land impracticable; to obviate which difficulty we purchased a large canoe and came down the Sangamon river in it. This is the time and manner of my entrance into Sangamon county. We found Offutt at Springfield, but learned from him that he had failed in getting a boat at Beardstown. This led to our hiring ourselves to him at $12. per month, each; and getting the timber out of the trees and building a boat at old Sangamon Town on the Sangamon river, seven miles northwest of Springfield, which boat we took to New Orleans, substantially upon the old contract.

The big trees were cut down, cut into logs and then taken down the river to a mill to be made into planking. The men lived in a shed which they had constructed. Lincoln did most of the cooking, except when kind neighbors invited the young men to dine. After about a month of hard labor, the cumbersome flatboat was completed. Offutt now agreed to pay them 50¢ a day plus $60 for the actual trip.

It was in connection with this boat that occurred the ludicrous incident of sewing up the hogs eyes. Offutt bought thirty odd large fat live hogs, but found difficulty in driving them from where he purchased them to the boat, and thereupon conceived the whim that he could sew up their eyes and drive them where he pleased. No sooner thought of than decided, he put his hands, including me at the job, which they completed—all but the driving. In their blind condition they could not be driven out of the lot or field they were in. This expedient failing, they were tied and hauled on carts to the boat. It was near the Sangamon river, within what is now Menard county.

The awkward craft began the initial stage of its journey down the Sangamon river in late April. Loaded with pork, corn, and live hogs, the flatboat soon encountered trouble. The receding flood waters had left the river shallow, and there were many timber obstructions and sand bars. At the little village of New Salem, the flatboat became stuck on Rutledge and Camron's mill dam. Water in the stern threatened to sink the flatboat. Lincoln went into the village and borrowed an auger from Henry Onstot, the cooper. When he returned to the flatboat, he ordered the cargo in stern unloaded so that the weight that remained in the forward part of the craft would cause it to right itself. Lincoln bored some holes in the forward part of the bottom, thus allowing the water to run out. Then, plugging the holes, Lincoln and the boatman were able to move the lightened boat over the dam. Residents of the village who had watched these proceedings from the river bank congratulated them and were particularly impressed with young Lincoln.

During this boat enterprise acquaintance with Offutt, who was previously an entire stranger, he conceived a liking for me and believing he could turn me to account, he contracted with me to act as clerk for him, on my return from New Orleans, in charge of a store and mill at New Salem, then in Sangamon, now in Menard county. Hanks had not gone to New Orleans, but having a family, and being likely to be detained from home longer than at first expected, had turned back from St. Louis. He is a first cousin of my mother. My father, with his own family and others mentioned, had, in pursuance of their intention, removed from Macon to Coles county.

The flatboat proceeded along the Sangamon river, into the Illinois, and then down the Mississippi to its destination, New Orleans. The many hours and days spent together on the crude craft enabled Denton Offutt to study the tall, serious young man, recently come from Indiana. Lincoln returned to Illinois by steamboat.

*Then came the Black-Hawk war; and I was
elected a Captain of Volunteers—a success
which gave me more pleasure than any I have
had since.*

BLACK HAWK WAR

I stopped indefinitely, and, for the first time, as it were,
by myself, at New Salem. This was in July, 1831. Here
I rapidly made acquaintances and friends. In less than a
year Offutt's business was failing—had almost failed—
when the Black Hawk war of 1832—broke out. I joined
a volunteer company, and to my own surprise, was elected
captain of it—a success which gave me more pleasure
than any I have had since. I went the campaign, served
near three months, met the ordinary hardships of such
an expedition, but was in no battle. I now own in Iowa,
the land upon which my own warrants for this service,
were located.

Lincoln had enlisted for thirty days to drive Black Hawk
and his band of Sac and Fox west of the Mississippi river. On
May 27, 1832, he was mustered out and re-enlisted as a private
in Captain Elijah Iles' company for twenty days. On June 16
he enlisted once more—this time for thirty days in Captain
Jacob M. Early's Independent Spy Corps. Before his enlist-
ment expired he wrote the mustering-out roll for the Com-

pany. Black Hawk had been defeated and captured, though through no direct effort of Lincoln's. After being mustered out in southern Wisconsin, Lincoln made his way back to New Salem on foot. The night before he left for Illinois, his horse was stolen. He arrived back in Illinois shortly before the election of members of the State Legislature.

He recalled his war experiences in a speech in Congress in 1848. He used the occasion to belittle the military reputation of the Democratic candidate for the presidency, Lewis Cass.

By the way, Mr. Speaker, did you know that I am a military hero? Yes sir; in the days of the Black Hawk War I fought, bled, and came away. Speaking of General Cass' career, reminds me of my own. I was not at Stillman's defeat, but I was about as near it, as Cass was to Hull's surrender; and, like him, I saw the place very soon afterwards. It is quite certain I did not break my sword, for I had none to break; but I bent a musket pretty badly on one occasion. If Cass broke his sword, the idea is, he broke it in desperation; I bent the musket by accident. If General Cass went in advance of me in picking whortleberries, I guess I surpassed him in charges upon the wild onions. If he saw any live, fighting Indians, it was more than I did; but I had a good many bloody struggles with the mosquitoes; and although I never fainted from loss of blood, I can truly say I was often very hungry.

Returning from the campaign, and encouraged by my great popularity among my immediate neighbors, I, the same year, ran for the Legislature and was beaten—my own precinct, however, casting its votes 277 for, and 7 against me—the only time I have been beaten by the people. And this too while I was an avowed [Henry] Clay man, and the precinct the autumn afterwards, giving a majority of 115 to General Jackson over Mr. Clay.

He had run eighth among thirteen candidates—only four were elected. The campaign, however, proved of inestimable value to him. It widened his acquaintance, gave him much needed experience in public speaking, and caused him to become aware of his political possibilities. It increased his confidence in himself. For the first time in his life, he was living in an organized community. It was here that he learned that if people liked you, and respected you, they might vote for you.

Legend has it that he courted the daughter of James Rutledge, the owner of the tavern at New Salem. For a brief time Lincoln did board at the tavern, and in the tiny village of only one hundred souls, Ann Rutledge and Abraham Lincoln would certainly have been friends. But the facts in this story do not support the romantic rumor. The facts are that this pretty twenty-two-year-old, blue-eyed girl was engaged to be married to John McNamar (McNeil), the partner of Samuel Hill, New Salem's leading merchant. He had returned east for a visit to New York where his family lived, and his lengthy absence began to cause some gossip. In the summer of 1835, at the Rutledge farm on Sand Ridge, seven miles north of New Salem, Ann contracted a disease—probably typhoid fever—and died after a short illness. It was not until almost thirty years later, that some hint of this supposed romance came to light. After Lincoln's death in 1865, his law partner, William H. Herndon, helped to circulate the story, but Lincoln scholars have never accepted it. To refute the story that Lincoln was so broken-hearted at Ann's death, that his friends were worried lest he destroy himself, there is the known incident that shortly thereafter he became infatuated with a Kentucky girl who had come to visit her sister in New Salem. Lincoln sent several letters to Mary Owens, and the friendship continued after he moved to Springfield, where it was finally terminated by mutual consent.

If you intend to go to work, there is no better place than right where you are; if you do not intend to go to work, you can not get along any where.

POSTMASTER AND SURVEYOR

He had failed in his first attempt to achieve elected office. He was out of work. It was a critical period for the young man. He thought a solution to his problems had come when he was offered an opportunity to purchase, by promissory note, Rowan Herndon's interest in a partnership in a general store with William F. Berry.

I was now without means and out of business, but was anxious to remain with my friends who had treated me with so much generosity, especially as I had nothing else-where to go to. I studied what I should do—thought of learning the blacksmith trade—thought of trying to study law—rather thought I could not succeed at that without a better education.

Before long, strangely enough, a man offered to sell and did sell, to me and another as poor as myself, an old stock of goods, upon credit. We opened as merchants; and that was the store. Of course we did nothing but get deeper and deeper in debt. I was appointed Postmaster at New Salem—the office being too insignificant, to make my politics an objection. The store winked out. The Surveyor of Sangamon, offered to depute to me that portion of his work which was within my part of the country. I accepted, procured a compass and chain, studied Flint, and Gibson a little, and went at it. This procured bread, and kept soul and body together.

As to an extra session of the Legislature,
I should know no better how to bring this
about, than to lift myself over a fence by
the straps of my boots.

ILLINOIS LEGISLATOR

Having made himself better known by his efforts as a surveyor and as the postmaster at New Salem, Lincoln determined to make another attempt at elective office.

The election of 1834 came, and I was then elected to the Legislature by the highest vote cast for any candidate. Major John T. Stuart, then in full practice of the law, was also elected. During the canvass, in a private conversation he encouraged me to study law. After the election I borrowed books of Stuart, took them home with me, and went at it in earnest. I studied with nobody. I still mixed in the surveying to pay board and clothing bills. When the Legislature met, the law books were dropped, but were then taken up again at the end of the session. I was re-elected in 1836, 1838, and 1840. I was not a candidate afterwards.

On March 3rd, 1837, by a protest entered upon the Illinois State Journal of that date, at pages 817 and 818, I, with Dan Stone, another representative of Sangamon, briefly defined my position on the slavery question; and so far as it goes, it was the same as now. In 1838, and 1840 my party in the Legislature voted for me as Speaker; but being in the minority, I was not elected. After 1840, I declined a re-election to the Legislature. I was on the Harrison electoral ticket in 1840, and on that of Clay in 1844, and spent much time and labor in both of those canvasses.

As a supporter of Henry Clay, he was a Whig in the Legislature, which had a Democratic majority. He had placed his belief in the injustice and evil of slavery into the record in order to condemn resolutions passed by the House attacking abolition societies.

The leading rule for the lawyer, as for the man of every other calling, is diligence. Leave nothing for to-morrow which can be done to-day. Never let your correspondence fall behind.

SPRINGFIELD LAWYER

In 1836, the post office at New Salem was closed and a facility opened in Petersburg, a village two miles to the north. This town would become the county seat for the new county which would be formed from the northern part of Sangamon. The days of New Salem were numbered, settlers began to leave for other localities which offered more promise.

In the autumn of 1836 I obtained a law license, and on April 15, 1837, removed to Springfield, and commenced the practice, my old friend, Stuart taking me into partnership.

He rode into Springfield on a borrowed horse; all of his possessions in two saddle-bags. He was befriended by a young Kentuckian, Joshua Fry Speed, who ran a general store. Speed invited the equally youthful lawyer-legislator to share his quarters above the store, without rent. Lincoln would later refer to Speed as "my most intimate friend"; it became the closest personal relationship he ever established with any man.

He continued his study and his reading, as he would all of his life. Years later he would advise a young man who wanted to make the law his career:

If you are resolutely determined to make a lawyer of yourself, the thing is more than half-done already. It is but a small matter whether you read *with* anybody or not. I did not read with anyone. Get the books, and read and study them till you understand them in their principal features; and that is the main thing. It is of no consequence to be in a large town while you are reading. I read at New Salem, which never had three hundred people living in it. The *books*, and your *capacity* for understanding them, are just the same in all places. Always bear in mind that your own resolution to succeed, is more important than any other one thing.

After a four-year law association with John T. Stuart, the partnership was dissolved and he became the junior partner of Stephen T. Logan, one of the most capable lawyers in the State. In 1844, this firm was dissolved, and on December 9 Lincoln became the senior partner of a law association with William H. Herndon. Lincoln and Herndon continued as a firm in the practice of the law until April 15, 1865.

Whatever woman may cast her lot with mine, should any ever do so, it is my intention to do all in my power to make her happy and contented; . . .

MARRIAGE TO MARY TODD

In 1837, the nineteen-year-old daughter of a prominent Kentuckian, Robert Smith Todd, came to Springfield to visit her sister, Elizabeth, who was married to Ninian W. Edwards. Two years later she returned to make it her permanent home. Mary Ann Todd and Abraham Lincoln met, and the two young people were attracted to one another. She was intelligent, well-informed politically, impulsive, possessed of a sense of humor that could be rather sharp, and at times, indicated a temper. He suggested marriage; they seemingly agreed, but then plans for a wedding were abandoned on January 1, 1841. Later the efforts of friends, and news of Joshua Speed's marriage, helped bring about a reconciliation of the couple.

In November, 1842, I was married to Mary, daughter of Robert S. Todd, of Lexington, Kentucky.

The Reverend Charles Dresser performed the ceremony, which took place in the Edwards home. Shortly thereafter Lincoln wrote to a fellow-lawyer:

Nothing new here, except my marrying, which to me is a matter of profound wonder.

To Speed he would soon write:

About the prospect of your having a namesake at our house, can't say, exactly yet.

I am forty-five years of age, and have a wife and three children, the oldest eleven years. My wife was born and raised at Lexington, Kentucky.

THE LINCOLN FAMILY

We have three living children, all sons—one was born in 1843, one in 1850, and one in 1853. We lost one, who was born in 1846.

The Lincolns had four sons in all—Robert Todd, Edward Baker, William Wallace, and Thomas "Tad." Eddie died in 1850, Willie in 1862, and Tad in 1871. Robert was the only son to attain maturity. He lived until 1926 and became a successful attorney, president of the Pullman Company, Secretary of War and Minister to Great Britain.

When he was away from his family, Lincoln's thoughts were always with them. His letters to Mary demonstrate his affection and concern.

In this troublesome world, we are never quite satisfied. When you were here, I thought you hindered me some in attending to business; but now, having nothing but business—no variety—it has grown exceedingly tasteless to me . . . I hate to stay in this old room by myself. I went yesterday to hunt the little plaid stockings, as you wished; but found . . . only one plaid pair of any sort that I thought would fit "Eddy's dear little feet." Are you entirely free from headache? That is good—good—considering it is the first spring you have been free from it since we were acquainted. I am afraid you will get so well, and fat, and young, as to want to be marrying again. Come on just as soon as you can. I want to see you, and our dear—*dear* boys very much. Everybody here wants to see our dear Bobby.

By the way, you do not intend to do without a girl, because the one you had has left you? Get another as soon as you can to take charge of the dear codgers. Father expected to see you all sooner; but let it pass; stay as long as you please, and come when you please. Kiss and love the dear rascals for me.

Mary and the boys were visiting her father and the Todd family in Lexington, Kentucky. His father and stepmother had settled in Charleston, Illinois, and from time to time he would provide some financial aid.

I very cheerfully send you the twenty dollars, which sum you say is necessary to save your land from sale. . . . Give my love to Mother, and all the connections.

Later, to his step-brother, John D. Johnston, he writes concerning his father's declining health.

I sincerely hope Father may yet recover his health; but at all events tell him to remember to call upon, and confide in, our great, and good, and merciful Maker; who will not turn away from him in any extremity. He notes the fall of a sparrow, and numbers the hairs on our heads; and He will not forget the dying man, who puts his trust in Him.

Being elected to Congress, though I am very
grateful to our friends, for having done it,
has not pleased me as much as I expected.

UNITED STATES CONGRESSMAN

In 1846 I was once elected to the lower House of Congress; commencing in December, 1847 and ending with
the inauguration of General Taylor, in March 1849. All
the battles of the Mexican War had been fought before I
took my seat in Congress, but the American army was still
in Mexico, and the treaty of peace was not fully and formally ratified till the June afterwards. Much has been said
of my course in Congress in regard to this war. A careful
examination of the Journals and Congressional Globe
show, that I voted for all the supply measures which
came up, and for all the measures in any way favorable to
the officers, soldiers, and their families, who conducted
the war through; with this exception that some of the
measures passed without yeas and nays, leaving no record
as to how particular men voted. The Journals and Globe
also show me voting that the war was unnecessarily and
unconstitutionally begun by the President of the United
States. This is the language of Mr. Ashmun's amendment,
for which I and nearly or quite all, other Whigs of the
House of Representatives voted. My reasons for the

opinion expressed by this vote were briefly that the President had sent General Taylor into an uninhabited part of the country belonging to Mexico, and not the United States and thereby had provoked the first act of hostility—in fact the commencement of the war; that the place, being the country bordering on the east bank of the Rio Grande, was inhabited by native Mexicans, born there under the Mexican government; and had never submitted to, nor been conquered by Texas, or the United States nor transferred to either by treaty—that although Texas claimed the Rio Grande as her boundary, Mexico had never recognized it, and neither Texas, nor the United States had ever enforced it—that there was a broad desert between that, and the country over which Texas had actual control—that the country where hostilities commenced, having once belonged to Mexico, must remain so, until it was somehow legally transferred, which had never been done.

I thought the act of sending an armed force among the Mexicans, was *unnecessary*, inasmuch as Mexico was in no way molesting, or menacing the United States or the people thereof; and that it was *unconstitutional*, because the power of levying war is vested in Congress, and not in the President. I thought the principal motive for the act, was to divert public attention from the surrender of "Fifty-four, forty, or fight" to Great Britain, on the Oregon boundary question.

The Congressman from the Illinois Seventh District did not serve with particular distinction. By agreement he had made a commitment in advance not to seek re-election. Perhaps his only action of significance was his support of an unsuccessful attempt to abolish slavery in the District of Columbia.

I was not a candidate for re-election. This was determined upon, and declared before I went to Washington, in accordance with an understanding among Whig friends, by which Colonel [John J.] Hardin, and Colonel [Edward D.] Baker each had previously served a single term in the same district.

In 1848, during my term in Congress, I advocated General Taylor's nomination for the Presidency, in opposition to all others, and also took an active part for his election, after his nomination—speaking a few times in Maryland, near Washington, several times in Massachusetts, and canvassing quite fully my own district in Illinois, which was followed by a majority in the district of over 1500 for General Taylor.

"A house divided against itself cannot stand." I believe this government cannot endure, permanently half slave and half free.

THE HOUSE DIVIDED

Upon my return from Congress I went into the practice of law. From 1849 to 1854, both inclusive, practiced law more assiduously than ever before. Always a Whig in politics, and generally on the Whig electoral tickets, making active canvasses. In 1854, my profession had almost superseded the thought of politics in my mind, when the Missouri Compromise aroused me as I had never been before.

The Missouri Compromise of 1820 had provided that slavery was to be abolished north of the line of 36° 30'. In 1854, Senator Stephen A. Douglas, leader of the Democratic party in Illinois, introduced his Kansas-Nebraska bill, the effect of which would be the repeal of the slavery restrictions of the Missouri Compromise. From the moment of the introduction of the bill, January 23, 1854, the controversy across the country became intense. Lincoln delivered great speeches on the subject in Springfield, Bloomington, and Peoria.

In the autumn of that year I took the stump with no broader political aim or object than to secure, if possible, the re-election of Honorable Richard Yates to Congress.

My speeches at once attracted a more marked audience than they had ever done before. As the canvass proceeded, I was drawn to different parts of the State, outside of Mr. Yates' district. I did not abandon the law, but gave my attention, by turns, to that and politics. The State agricultural fair was at Springfield that year, and Douglas was announced to speak there.

Lincoln answered Douglas in Springfield. The *Illinois Journal* for October 5, 1854, commented, "His remarks about Union saving were sound and patriotic, and his appeal to the Southern States for moderation and forebearance, fraternal and eloquent. He did not set so much store on the restoration of the Missouri Compromise by act of legislation, as he did on the immediate and effectual restoration of it by popular sentiment. This last was possible. Let the decided demonstration of the Free States secure it. That being done, the Union would again be safe and the people happy."

In February, 1855, Lincoln failed to secure election by the Illinois State Legislature to the United States Senate, finally throwing his votes to Lyman Trumbull, who was elected on the tenth ballot.

In 1856, Lincoln became totally involved in the fortunes of the new Republican party, and on May 29th, in Bloomington, delivered his now famous "Lost Speech," on the occasion of the organization of the party in Illinois.

The *Weekly North-Western Gazette*, on July 29th quoted Lincoln as saying, "The Supreme Court of the United States is the tribunal to decide such questions [laws restricting slavery], and we will submit to its decisions . . ." Lincoln's stated position on the Dred Scott decision did not agree with this statement—he felt that the people should abide by the decision until a reversal could be obtained from the court. The Democrats were quick to point to what they claimed to be his contradictory position on this matter. He referred to it.

In the canvass of 1856, I made over fifty speeches, no one of which, so far as I remember, was put in print. One of them was made at Galena, but I have no recollection of any part of it being printed; nor do I remember whether in that speech I said anything about a Supreme Court decision. I may have spoken on that subject; and some of the newspapers may have reported me as saying what is now ascribed to me; but I think I could not have expressed myself as represented.

What I have done since is pretty well known.

He was right. Abraham Lincoln was now the leading Republican of Illinois, taking the same position he had previously held as Whig leader of the State. On June 19, 1856, when the first Republican National Convention was held at Philadelphia, he received 110 votes for the vice-presidential nomination—his name was becoming widely known throughout the North. He campaigned unsuccessfully for John C. Fremont, the Republican candidate, who was defeated by James Buchanan.

I suppose that Judge Douglas will claim in a little while, that he is the inventor of the idea that the people should govern themselves; that nobody ever thought of such a thing until he brought it forward.

DEBATES WITH DOUGLAS

Lincoln was the "first and only choice" for the Republican senatorial nomination in 1858. He welcomed the opportunity to be pitted against Stephen A. Douglas, who more than any other man was responsible for the repeal of the Missouri Compromise. On July 24, he challenged the "Little Giant" to a series of debates, asking in a letter, "Will it be agreeable to you to make an arrangement for you and myself to divide time, and address the same audiences during the present canvass?" Beginning at Ottawa on August 21, and closing at Alton on October 15, the debates aroused national interest. Capitalizing on a growing split in the Democratic ranks, Lincoln repeatedly referred to Douglas' indifference to the moral question of the right and wrong of slavery. At the second debate at Freeport, he forced Douglas to compromise himself, by taking a position which gained votes in Illinois, but which offended the South.

I am opposed to the acquisition of any more territory unless slavery is first prohibited therein, my answer is such that I could add nothing by way of illustration, or making myself better understood, than the answer which I have placed in writing.

Now in all this, the Judge [Douglas] has me and he has me on the record. I suppose he has flattered himself that I was really entertaining one set of opinions for one place and another set for another place—that I was afraid to say at one place what I uttered at another.

Lincoln then proceeded to ask Douglas to answer a series of questions, the second of which was the key to the entire debate.

Can the people of a United States territory, in any lawful way, against the wish of any citizen of the United States, exclude slavery from its limits prior to the formation of a state constitution?

Douglas in reply stated that, in his opinion, the people of a territory could, "by lawful means, exclude slavery from their limits prior to the formation of a state constitution. . . . It matters not what way the Supreme Court may hereafter decide as to the abstract question whether slavery may or may not go into a territory under the Constitution, the people have the lawful means to introduce it or exclude it as they please, for the reason that slavery cannot exist a day or an hour anywhere, unless it is supported by local police regulations."

He ended the campaign where it began—in Springfield.

I have said that in some respects the contest has been painful to me. Myself, and those with whom I act have been constantly accused of a purpose to destroy the Union; and bespattered with every imaginable odious epithet; and some who were friends, as it were but yesterday have made themselves most active in this. I have cultivated patience, and made no attempt at a retort.

Ambition has been ascribed to me. God knows how sincerely I prayed from the first that this field of ambition might not be opened. I claim no insensibility to political honors; but today could the Missouri restriction be restored, and the whole slavery question replaced on the ground of "toleration" by necessity where it exists, with unyielding hostility to the spread of it, on principle, I would, in consideration, gladly agree, that Judge Douglas should never be *out*, and I never *in*, an office as long as both or either, live.

Later he would say:

The cause of civil liberty must not be surrendered at the end of *one*, or even *one hundred* defeats. Douglas had the ingenuity to be supported in the late contest both as the best means to *break down*, and to *uphold* the Slave interest. No ingenuity can keep those antagonistic elements in harmony long.

In the election of November, Lincoln received a majority of the votes, but the unequal division of the legislative districts gave Douglas the election in the Legislature. Though defeated, Abraham Lincoln had become a national political figure.

He made a brief comment on his appearance at this time.

If any personal description of me is thought desirable, it may be said, I am, in height, six feet, four inches, nearly; lean in flesh, weighing on an average, one hundred and eighty pounds; dark complexion, with coarse black hair, and grey eyes—no other marks or brands recollected.

*As to the Presidential nomination, claiming
no greater exemption from selfishness than is
common, I still feel that my whole aspiration
should be . . . to be placed anywhere or
nowhere as may appear most likely to advance
our cause.*

NOMINATION FOR PRESIDENT

In 1859 he made speeches in Indiana, Iowa, Ohio, and Wisconsin, carrying his ideas to the voters in these states. He was being mentioned in many areas as a presidential possibility, and in a letter to Senator Trumbull he referred to his ambition.

I will be entirely frank. The taste *is* in my mouth a little; and this no doubt, disqualifies me, to some extent, to form correct opinions.

It was as a presidential possibility that he was invited to speak in New York on February 27, 1860, at the Cooper Institute. The invitation originated with the Young Men's Republican Union. His speech was delivered with sincerity and dignity and was well received. He also spoke in New Hampshire, Connecticut, and Rhode Island before he returned to Illinois. He was in touch with political leaders all across the North, and there were practical problems to consider.

I cannot enter the ring on the money basis—first, because, in the main, the use of money is wrong; and secondly, I have not, and can not get, the money. I say in the main, the use of money is wrong; but for certain objects, in a political contest, the use of some, is both right and indispensable.

My name is new in the field; and I suppose I am not the *first* choice of a great many. Our policy, then, is to give no offense to others—leave them in a mood to come to us, if they shall be compelled to give up their first love. This, too, is dealing justly with all, and leaving us in a mood to support heartily whoever shall be nominated.

On May 10, 1860, the Illinois State Republican Convention, meeting in Decatur, adopted the resolution, "That Abraham Lincoln is the choice of the Republican party of Illinois for the Presidency, and the delegates from this state are instructed to use all honorable means to secure his nomination by the Chicago Convention, and to vote as a unit for him."

John Hanks, his cousin, carried two rails into the convention hall. Supported between the rails was a banner reading, "Abraham Lincoln, The Rail Candidate for President in 1860." The banner also mentioned that these rails were two of the 3,000 made in 1830 by Lincoln and others in Macon County. He was now the "Rail Splitter" candidate.

First then, I think the Illinois delegation will be unanimous for me at the start; and no other delegation will. A few individuals in other delegations would like to go for me at the start, but may be restrained by their colleagues. It is represented to me, by men who ought to know, that the whole of Indiana might not be difficult to get. You know how it is in Ohio. I am certainly not the first choice there; and yet I have not heard that anyone makes any positive objection to me. It is just so everywhere so far as I can perceive.

The Republicans assembled for their national convention in Chicago, on May 16th. Lincoln's managers, Judge David Davis, of Bloomington, and Norman B. Judd, of Chicago, the state chairman, with great skill, worked with consummate effectiveness in persuading key delegations to support their candidate. Where delegations were pledged to favorite sons, they solicited the votes on subsequent ballots. On May 18th, on the third ballot, Abraham Lincoln was nominated for President of the United States, winning over William H. Seward, of New York; Simon Cameron, of Pennsylvania; Salmon P. Chase, of Ohio; and Edward Bates, of Missouri. Hannibal Hamlin, of Maine, was selected as candidate for Vice President. Lincoln wrote at once to the president of the convention, George Ashmun, of Massachusetts.

Deeply, and even painfully sensible of the great responsibility I could almost wish had fallen upon some one of the far more eminent men and experienced statesmen whose distinguished names were before the Convention, I shall . . . consider more fully the resolutions of the Convention, . . . and without unreasonable delay, respond to you, Mr. Chairman, in writing—not doubting now, that the platform will be found satisfactory, and the nomination gratefully accepted.

In his formal letter of acceptance, as he would on many future occasions, Lincoln invoked the aid of a higher power.

I accept the nomination tendered me by the Convention over which you presided, . . . imploring the assistance of Divine Providence, and with due regard to the views and feelings of all who were represented in the convention; to the rights of all the states, and territories, and the people of the nation; to the inviolability of the Constitution, and the perpetual union, harmony, and prosperity of all, I am most happy to co-operate for the practical success of the principles declared by the convention.

If any of the other candidates had been elected I think it would have been altogether becoming and proper for all to have joined in showing honor, quite as well to the office, and the country, as to the man.

PRESIDENTIAL ELECTION

As Lincoln had predicted, the antagonistic elements of the Democratic party could not be kept in harmony. In the campaign that followed, the Democrats split, North and South. He did not make any speeches during the campaign. To an old friend he surveyed his election prospects.

We do not know what a day may bring forth; but today, it looks as if the Chicago ticket will be elected. I think the chances were more than equal that we could have beaten the Democracy *united*. Divided, as it is, its chance appears indeed very slim. But great is Democracy in resources; and it may yet give its fortunes a turn. It is under great temptation to do something; but what can it do which was not thought of, and found impracticable, at Charleston and Baltimore? The signs are now that Douglas and Breckinridge will each have a ticket in every state. They are driven to this to keep up their bombastic claims of *nationality*, and to avoid the charge of *sectionalism* which they have so much lavished upon us.

The Northern Democrats selected Stephen A. Douglas, of Illinois, and Herschel V. Johnson, of Georgia, as their candidates. The Southern Democrats chose John C. Breckinridge, of Kentucky, and Joseph Lane, of Oregon, for President and Vice President. The Constitutional Union Party, which tried to ignore the slavery question, nominated John Bell, of Tennessee, and Edward Everett, of Massachusetts.

To those who urged him to state his position and views, he wrote a series of similar letters, explaining his silence.

Your suggestion that I, in a certain event, shall write a letter, setting forth my conservative views and intentions, is certainly a very worthy one. But would it do any good? If I were to labor a month, I could not express my conservative views and intentions more clearly and strongly, than they are expressed in our platform, and in my many speeches already in print, and before the public. And yet even you, who do occasionally speak of me in terms of personal kindness, give no prominence to these oft-repeated expressions of conservative views and intentions; . . . If what I have already said has failed to convince you, no repetition of it would convince you.

For the good men of the South—and I regard the majority of them as such—I have no objection to repeat seventy and seven times. But I have *bad* men also to deal with, both North and South—men who are eager for something new upon which to base new misrepresentations—men who would like to frighten me, or, at least, to fix upon me the character of timidity and cowardice. They would seize upon almost any letter I could write, as being an "*awful coming down*." I intend keeping my eye upon these gentlemen, and to not unnecessarily put any weapons in their hands.

On November 6th, Abraham Lincoln was elected President of the United States. He carried every Northern free state but New Jersey. The vote in the electoral college was: Lincoln 180, John C. Breckinridge 72, John Bell 39, and Stephen A. Douglas 12.

I am leaving you on an errand of national
importance, attended, as you are aware,
with considerable difficulties. Let us
believe, as some poet has expressed it:—
Behind the cloud the sun is still shining.

FAREWELL TO SPRINGFIELD

He had not spoken during the campaign, but he broke his
silence during the period between his election and his inauguration. Meanwhile the secession movement was sweeping
through the South. On December 20th, South Carolina
seceded from the Union. In January, 1861, Mississippi,
Florida, Alabama, Georgia, and Louisiana followed. On February 1st, Texas voted for secession also. On February 4th
representatives of six states (Texas was not represented) met
in Montgomery, Alabama, to form a provisional government
for the seceded states. A constitution was adopted, patterned
on that of the United States (with the exception of the provisions recognizing and protecting slavery), and Jefferson
Davis of Mississippi was selected as President of the government of the Confederate States of America.

   Lincoln tried to calm the fears of the South in a letter to
Alexander H. Stephens, of Georgia, an old friend who was to
become Vice President of the Confederacy.

Do the people of the South really entertain fears that a Republican administration would, *directly*, or *indirectly*, interfere with their slaves, or with them about their slaves? If they do, I wish to assure you, as once a friend, and still, I hope, not an enemy, that there is no cause for such fears.

The South would be in no more danger in this respect, than it was in the days of Washington. I suppose, however, this does not meet the case. You think slavery is *right* and ought to be extended; while we think it is *wrong* and ought to be restricted. That I suppose is the rub. It certainly is the only substantial difference between us.

On the morning of February 11, 1861, in a drizzling rain, he bid farewell to Springfield and Illinois. More than a thousand of his friends and fellow citizens came to the Great Western station to say goodbye. For almost a half-hour he shook hands with men and women, many of whom he had known for twenty-five years. He boarded the train that was to take him to Washington, and spoke from the rear platform.

My friends—No one, not in my situation, can appreciate my feeling of sadness at this parting. To this place, and the kindness of these people, I owe everything. Here I have lived a quarter of a century, and have passed from a young to an old man. Here my children have been born, and one is buried. I now leave, not knowing when, or whether ever, I may return, with a task before me greater than that which rested upon Washington. Without the assistance of that Divine Being, who ever attended him, I cannot succeed. With that assistance I cannot fail. Trusting in Him, who can go with me, and remain with you and be everywhere for good, let us confidently hope that all will yet be well. To His care commending you, as I hope in your prayers you will commend me, I bid you an affectionate farewell.

En route to Washington his twelve-day journey took him to many stopping places. He made dozens of speeches, including one in Philadelphia at Independence Hall.

I have often pondered over the dangers which were incurred by the men who assembled here and adopted that Declaration of Independence—I have pondered over the toils that were endured by the officers and soldiers of the army, who achieved that Independence. I have often inquired of myself, what great principle or idea it was that kept this Confederacy so long together. It was mother land; but something in that declaration giving liberty, not alone to the people of this country, but hope to the world for all future time. It was that which gave promise that in due time the weights should be lifted from the shoulders of all men, and that not the mere matter of the separation of the colonies from the *all* should have an equal chance. This is the sentiment embodied in that Declaration of Independence.

Now, my friends, can this country be saved upon that basis? If it can, I will consider myself one of the happiest men in the world if I can help to save it. If it can't be saved upon that principle, it will be truly awful. But, if this country cannot be saved without giving up that principle—I was about to say I would rather be assassinated on this spot than to surrender it.

In compliance with a custom as old as the government itself, I appear before you to address you briefly, and to take, in your presence, the oath prescribed by the Constitution of the United States, . . .

FIRST INAUGURAL

On March 4th, on the east portico of the Capitol, Chief Justice Roger B. Taney administered the oath of office to Abraham Lincoln, who thus became the Sixteenth President of the United States. In his inaugural address he pleaded for the maintenance of the Union.

Physically speaking we cannot separate. We cannot remove our respective sections from each other, nor build an impassable wall between them. . . . Can aliens make treaties easier than friends can make laws? Can treaties be more faithfully enforced between aliens, than laws can among friends? Suppose you go to war, you cannot fight always; and when, after much loss on both sides, and no gain on either, you cease fighting, the identical old question, as to terms of intercourse, are again upon you.

This country, with its institutions, belongs to the people who inhabit it. Whenever they shall grow weary of the existing government, they can exercise their *con-*

stitutional right of amending it, or their *revolutionary* right to dismember, or overthrow it. . . .

Why should there not be a patient confidence in the ultimate justice of the people? Is there any better, or equal hope, in the world? In our present differences, is either party without faith of being in the right? If the Almighty Ruler of nations, with his eternal truth and justice, be on your side of the North, or on yours of the South, that truth, and that justice, will surely prevail by the judgment of that great tribunal, the American people.

In *your* hands, my dissatisfied fellow-countrymen, and not in *mine*, is the momentous issue of civil war. The government will not assail *you*. You can have no conflict, without being yourselves the aggressors. *You* have no oath registered in Heaven to destroy the government, while *I* shall have the most solemn one to "preserve, protect and defend" it.

I am loath to close. We are not enemies, but friends. We must not be enemies. Though passion may have strained, it must not break our bonds of affection. The mystic chords of memory, stretching from every battlefield, and patriot grave, to every living heart and hearthstone, all over this broad land, will yet swell the chorus of the Union, when again touched, as surely they will be, by the better angels of our nature.

But civil war could not be avoided, and on April 12th the Confederate forces of South Carolina fired on Fort Sumter, in Charleston harbor, and all talk of reconciliation, all hope of peace, was ended. On April 15, 1861, the new President of the United States issued a proclamation.

Whereas the laws of the United States have been for some time past, and now are opposed, and the execution thereof obstructed, in the States of South Carolina, Georgia, Alabama, Florida, Mississippi, Louisiana and Texas, by combinations too powerful to be suppressed by the ordinary course of judicial proceedings, or by the powers vested in the Marshals by law.

Now therefore, I, Abraham Lincoln, President of the United States, in virtue of the power in me vested by the Constitution, and the laws, have thought fit to call forth, and hereby do call forth, the militia of the several States of the Union, to the aggregate number of seventy-five thousand, in order to suppress said combinations, and to cause the laws to be duly executed.

Virginia, Arkansas, and Tennessee completed the parade of states to secede. Maryland, Missouri, and Kentucky would remain in the Union, though divided in their loyalty. Though talk of war had been in the air for months, the people were none the less stunned. And there were those who wanted peace at any price, such as the citizens of Baltimore who called on the President. His reply was stern.

You, gentlemen, come here to me and ask for peace on any terms, and yet have no word of condemnation for those who are making war on us. You express great horror of bloodshed, and yet would not lay a straw in the way of those who are making war on us. The rebels attack Fort Sumter, and your citizens attack troops sent to the defense of the Government, and the lives and property in Washington, and yet you would have me break my oath and surrender the Government without a blow. There is no Washington in that—no Jackson in that—no manhood or honor in that. I have no desire to invade the South; but I must have troops to defend this Capital. Geographically it lies surrounded by the soil of Maryland; and mathematically the necessity exists that they should come over her territory. Our men are not moles, and can't dig under the earth; they are not birds, and can't fly through the air. There is no way but to march across, and that they must do. But in doing this there is no need of collision. Keep your rowdies in Baltimore and there will be no bloodshed. Go home and tell your people that if they will not attack us, we well not attack them; but if they do attack us, we will return it, and that severely.

*And upon this act, sincerely believed to be
an act of justice, warranted by the Constitution, upon military necessity, I invoke the
considerate judgment of mankind, and the
gracious favor of Almighty God.*

EMANCIPATION PROCLAMATION

Civil War had come to the United States. Before it was over,
four years later, it would be the bloodiest, costliest war in
terms of human lives in our history. Six hundred thousand
men would give their lives to preserve their own principles of
freedom. To Abraham Lincoln had come the responsibility
of leading the nation through the years of this fratricidal conflict, which some of his critics called "Mr. Lincoln's War." It
was not an easy task. His leading opponents in the Republican
convention were now in his Cabinet. There was little agreement by his so-called advisors on the course of action to be
taken. Several members of the Cabinet privately believed that
they should be in his position, and most personally believed
they could do a better job than Lincoln. He had major problems with his military leaders. When he came to office,
venerable Winfield Scott was commanding officer of the
United States. Before the war came to a successful conclusion,
Lincoln would suffer through the commands of George B.
McClellan, John Pope, Ambrose E. Burnside, Joseph Hooker,

and George G. Meade, until he found the right general in a slight, unkempt, cigar-smoking fighter from the West, named Ulysses S. Grant.

He had many critics, both in and out of government. To all of them and to the nation, he gave his answer in his Annual Message to Congress in 1862.

We can succeed only by concert. It is not "can *any* of us *imagine* better?" but "can we *all* do better?" Object whatsoever is possible, still the question recurs "can we do better?" The dogmas of the quiet past, are inadequate to the stormy present. The occasion is piled high with difficulty, and we must rise with the occasion. As our case is new, so we must think anew, and act anew. We must disenthrall ourselves, and then we shall save our country.

Fellow-citizens, *we* cannot escape history. We of this Congress and this administration, will be remembered in spite of ourselves. No personal significance, or insignificance, can spare one or another of us. The fiery trial through which we pass, will light us down, in honor or dishonor, to the latest generation. We say we are for the Union. The world will not forget that we say this. We know how to save the Union. The world knows we do know how to save it. We—even *we here*—hold the power, and bear the responsibility. In *giving* freedom to the *slave*, we *assure* freedom to the *free*—honorable alike in what we give, and what we preserve. We shall nobly save, or meanly lose, the last best, hope of earth. Other means may succeed; this could not fail. The way is plain, peaceful, generous, just—a way which, if followed, the world will forever applaud, and God must forever bless.

As the war progressed, Lincoln had come to realize that the preservation of the Union, important though it was, was not the only issue at stake. He proposed various schemes to deal with the slavery question; realizing that abroad the North lacked complete sympathy, since in effect we "sought to put down the rebellion with the left hand, while supporting slavery with the right hand." A plan of colonization in Africa failed to gain support; and a scheme of voluntary emancipation with compensation to slave owners never obtained Congressional support.

In the summer of 1862, he called his Cabinet together and advised them of his next course of action. He read the first draft of the Emancipation Proclamation to his department heads. It called for preliminary moves for the freedom of the slaves by presidential edict. This was a change in policy; heretofore he had been firm in stating that the Government would not interfere with the institution where it existed. All of the Cabinet members agreed to the expediency of the measure. Seward, Secretary of State, however, felt that the proclamation should not be issued until such a time as it could be coupled with news of military success on the part of the North. Lincoln agreed, and the announcement waited for news of victory. In August, the Union forces under General Pope were defeated by the Confederates led by Robert E. Lee—the disaster at Second Bull Run certainly did not provide the proper climate for the Presidential statement. In September, however, military matters took a turn for the better. The Union forces halted Lee's invasion of Maryland in a bloody battle at Antietam Creek, near Sharpsburg. It was enough of a victory to enable the President to issue his proclamation on September 22nd.

I, Abraham Lincoln, President of the United States of America, and Commander-in-Chief of the Army and Navy thereof, do hereby proclaim and declare that hereafter, as heretofore, the war will be prosecuted for the object of practically restoring the constitutional relation between the United States, and each of the states, and the people thereof, in which states that relation is, or may be suspended, or disturbed. . . .

That on the first day of January in the year of our Lord, one thousand eight hundred and sixty-three, all persons held as slaves within any state, or designated part of a state, the people whereof shall then be in rebellion against the United States shall be then, thenceforward, and forever free . . .

Lincoln, in effect, was offering the rebellious states a choice—return to the Union before January 1, 1863, or have your slaves freed. His order also made every advance of the Union army into a slave state a march of liberation. With this single action, he changed the character of the war, and also eliminated any possible chance of foreign intervention, since action now by another nation would be interpreted as support of slavery against the emancipation policies of the North. There was some criticism, and his reply was prompt and unequivocal.

I never did ask more, nor ever was willing to accept less, than for all the States, and the people thereof, to take and hold their places, and their rights, in the Union, under the Constitution of the United States. For this alone have I felt authorized to struggle; and I seek neither more nor less now. Still, to use a coarse, but an expressive figure, broken eggs cannot be mended. I have issued the Emancipation Proclamation, and I can not retract it.

After the commencement of hostilities I struggled nearly a year and a half to get along without touching the "institution"; and when finally I conditionally determined to touch it, I gave a hundred days fair notice of my purpose, to all the States and people within which time they could have turned it wholly aside, by simply again becoming good citizens of the United States. They chose to disregard it, and I made the pre-emptory proclamation of what appeared to me to be a military necessity. And being made, it must stand.

I sincerely wish war was an easier and pleasanter business than it is; but it does not admit of holidays.

COMMANDER-IN-CHIEF

The bloody war continued. In December, 1862, the Union army under General Burnside suffered a disastrous defeat at Fredericksburg in Virginia. It was obvious to the President that he needed a new commander for the Army of the Potomac. The most likely choice, Joseph Hooker, was handsome and hard fighting. He also talked too much, and tended to criticize his superiors. It was also rumored that he was a heavy drinker. Despite the misgivings he had, Lincoln gave the command to Hooker. He tried to advise his commander much as a father would a headstrong son.

General. I have placed you at the head of the Army of the Potomac. Of course I have done this upon what appear to me to be sufficient reasons. And yet I think it best for you to know that there are some things in regard to which, I am not quite satisfied with you. I believe you to be a brave and a skillful soldier, which of course I like. I also believe you do not mix politics with your profession, in which you are right. You have confidence in yourself, which is a valuable, if not an indispensable quality. You are ambitious, which, within reasonable bounds, does good rather than harm. But I think that during General Burnside's command of the army, you have taken counsel of your ambition, and thwarted him as much as you could, in which you did a great wrong to the country, and to a most meritorious and honorable brother officer. I have heard, in such a way as to believe it, of your recently saying that both the army and the government needed a dictator. Of course it was not *for* this, but in spite of it, that I have given you the command. Only those generals who gain successes, can set up dictators. What I now ask of you is military success, and I will risk the dictatorship. The government will support you to the utmost of its ability, which is neither more nor less than it has done and will do for all commanders. I much fear that the spirit which you have aided to infuse into the army, of criticizing their commander, and withholding confidence from him, will now turn upon you. I shall assist you as far as I can, to put it down. Neither you, nor Napoleon, if he were alive again, could get any good out of an army, while such a spirit prevails in it.

And now, beware of rashness. Beware of rashness, but with energy, and sleepless vigilence, go forward, and give us victories.

In the West, Ulysses S. Grant's objective was Vicksburg, Mississippi. As long as the South held it, the Mississippi river was closed to the Union Army. Through the winter of 1862–1863 and into the spring and summer the campaign against Vicksburg was pushed by Grant. Finally, on July 4, Vicksburg fell, and the Mississippi was in the hands of the Union. Lincoln had entertained doubts about some features of Grant's campaign. He admits his error in a letter to the General.

I do not remember that you and I ever met personally. I write this now as a grateful acknowledgment for the almost inestimable service you have done the country. I wish to say a word further. When you first reached the vicinity of Vicksburg, I thought you should do, what you finally did—march the troops across the neck, run the batteries with the transports, and thus go below; and I never had any faith, except a general hope that you knew better than I, that the Yazoo Pass expedition, and the like, could succeed. When you got below, and took Port Gibson, Grand Gulf, and vicinity, I thought you should go down the river and join General Banks; and when you turned northward east of the Big Black, I feared it was a mistake. I now wish to make the personal acknowledgment that you were right and I was wrong.

*I expected to see you here at Cabinet
meeting, and to say something about going
to Gettysburg. There will be a train to
take and return us.*

GETTYSBURG ADDRESS

Despite the encouragement and support of the President,
Hooker seemed to lose confidence in himself, and it was the
Confederates, Robert E. Lee and "Stonewall" Jackson, who
seized the initiative. On the morning of May 2, 1863, Jackson's Confederates surprised Hooker at Chancellorsville, and
by May 6th the Union army, defeated and demoralized, had
withdrawn to Fredericksburg. The cost to the South was
severe, also—Jackson was mortally wounded and died a
week later.

Lincoln was worried about the morale of the Army of the
Potomac, and in letters to General Hooker, expressed his fears,
and at the same time, offered some advice.

Have you already in your mind a plan wholly, or par-
tially formed? If you have, prosecute it without interfer-
ence from me. If you have not, please inform me, so that
I, incompetent as I may be, can try to assist in the formation of some plan for the army. . . . It does not now appear probable to me that you can gain anything by an
early renewal of the attempt to cross the Rappahannock.

I therefore shall not complain, if you do no more for a time, than to keep the enemy at bay, and out of other mischief, by menaces and occasional cavalry raids, if practicable; and to put your own army in good condition again. Still, if in your own clear judgment, you can renew the attack successfully, I do not mean to restrain you. Bearing upon this last point, I must tell you I have some painful intimations that some of your corps and division commanders are not giving you their entire confidence. This would be ruinous, if true; . . .

Late in June 1863, Lee moved the war north by invading Pennsylvania. On June 28th Hooker was relieved of command and replaced by Major General George G. Meade. During the first three days of July, the Union and Confederate forces clashed at Gettysburg. Until late on the second day, the Confederates seemed to be gaining the field. Then the tide turned, and on the third day the South was repulsed. Losses for both sides were heavy; but for the South they were irreplaceable. Though the war would continue for almost two more years, the victory at Gettysburg, plus the fall of Vicksburg, made eventual Union success inevitable.

When the battle of Gettysburg was over, more than 7,000 soldiers from both armies lay dead on the battlefield. The Governor of Pennsylvania, with the cooperation of the governors of the other seventeen northern states involved in the battle, arranged for the creation of a corporation to establish a military cemetery on the site. Thursday, November 19, 1863, was agreed upon as the dedication date, and Edward Everett, of Massachusetts, was invited to deliver the dedicatory oration. He was one of the foremost orators in the country, a Phi Beta Kappa, a professor of Greek at Harvard, and he was later to be president of that institution, a member of Congress, United States senator, minister to Great Britain, and secretary of state. On November 2, Lincoln was invited "To be present and participate in these ceremonies, which will doubtless be very imposing and solemnly impressive. It is the desire that after the oration, you as Chief Executive of the Nation, formally set apart these grounds to their sacred use by a few appropriate remarks . . ."

The President left Washington at noon on Wednesday, November 18, and it was evening when he arrived at Gettysburg. A number of military bands were in the city, and one of them serenaded Lincoln, who responded with a brief speech.

I appear before you fellow-citizens, merely to thank you for this compliment. The inference is a very fair one that you would hear me for a little while at least, were I to commence to make a speech. I do not appear before you for the purpose of doing so, and for several substantial reasons. The most substantial of these is that I have no speech to make.

At 10 A.M. the next morning there was a procession to the cemetery. Several thousand spectators were already there. After a prayer by the Chaplain of the House of Representatives, the Marine Band played, and then Everett spoke. His speech was most eloquent and lasted for almost two hours. All agree that it was a masterful work. Reporters commented that Lincoln listened intently. An ode was sung and then the Provost Marshal of the District of Columbia introduced the President of the United States. Then he spoke, reading his remarks.

Four score and seven years ago our fathers brought forth on this continent, a new nation, conceived in Liberty, and dedicated to the proposition that all men are created equal.

Now we are engaged in a great civil war, testing

whether that nation, or any nation so conceived and so dedicated, can long endure. We are met on a great battlefield of that war. We have come to dedicate a portion of that field, as a final resting place for those who here gave their lives that that nation might live. It is altogether fitting and proper that we should do this.

But in a larger sense, we can not dedicate—we can not consecrate—we can not hallow—this ground. The brave men, living and dead, who struggled here, have consecrated it, far above our poor power to add or detract. The world will little note, nor long remember what we say here, but it can never forget what they did here. It is for us the living, rather, to be dedicated here to the unfinished work which they who fought here have thus far so nobly advanced. It is rather for us to be here dedicated to the great task remaining before us—that from these honored dead we take increased devotion to that cause for which they gave the last full measure of devotion— that we here highly resolve that these dead shall not have died in vain—that this nation, under God, shall have a new birth of freedom—and that government of the people, by the people, for the people, shall not perish from the earth.

The day after the address, Edward Everett wrote to the President: "Permit me . . . to express my great admiration of the thoughts expressed by you, with such eloquent simplicity and appropriateness, at the consecration of the cemetery. I should be glad, if I could flatter myself that I came as near to the central ideas of the occasion in two hours, as you did in two minutes."

Lincoln's reply the same day was characteristic.

Your kind note of today is received. In our respective parts yesterday, you could not have been excused to make a short address, nor I a long one. I am pleased to know that in your judgment, the little I did say was not entirely a failure.

Having served four years in the depths of
a great and yet unended national peril, I can
view this call to a second term, in nowise
more flattering to myself, than as an expression
of public judgment, that I may better finish
a difficult work, . . .

SECOND INAUGURAL

Though the Union fortunes had improved, the people of the North were weary of war. In July, 1863, protests against the draft in New York City resulted in riots with several hundred deaths. To an old friend in Illinois, he wrote in answer to an invitation that he attend a meeting to be held in Springfield "of all those who maintain unconditional devotion to the Union."

It would be very agreeable to me, to thus meet my old friends, at my own home; but I cannot just now, be absent from here, so long as a visit there, would require.

There are those who are dissatisfied with me. To such I would say: You desire peace; and you blame me that we do not have it. But how can we attain it? There are but three conceivable ways. First, to suppress the rebellion by force of arms. This, I am trying to do. Are you for it? If you are, so far we are agreed. If you are not for it, a second way is, to give up the Union. I am against this. Are you for it? If you are, you should say so plainly. If you are not for *force*, nor yet for *dissolution*, there only remains some imaginable *compromise*. I do not believe any compromise, embracing the maintenance of the Union, is now possible. All I learn, leads to a directly opposite belief. The strength of the rebellion is its military—its army. That army dominates all the country, and all the people within its range. Any offer of terms made by any man or men within that range, in opposition to that army, is simply nothing for the present; because such man or men, have no power whatever to enforce their side of a compromise, if one were made with them.

I thought that in your struggle for the Union, to whatever extent the Negroes should cease helping the enemy, to that extent it weakened the enemy in resistance to you. Do you think differently? I thought that whatever Negroes can be got to do as soldiers, leaves just so much less for white soldiers to do, in saving the Union. Does it appear otherwise to you? But Negroes, like other people, act upon motives. Why should they do anything for us, if we will do nothing for them? If they stake their lives for us, they must be prompted by the strongest motive—even the promise of freedom. And the promise being made, must be kept.

The signs look better. The Father of Waters again goes unvexed to the sea. . . . And while those who have cleared the great river may well be proud, even that is not all. It is hard to say anything has been more bravely, and well done, than at Antietam, Murfreesboro, Gettysburg, and on many fields of lesser note. . . . Thanks to all. For the great republic—for the principle it lives by, and keeps alive—for man's vast future—thanks to all.

Peace does not appear so distant as it did. I hope it will come soon, and come to stay; and so come as to be worth the keeping in all future time. It will then have been proved that, among free men, there can be no successful appeal from the ballot to the bullet; and that they who take such appeal are sure to lose their case, and pay the cost.

In June, 1864, the Republicans, and some former Democrats, meeting in convention in Baltimore, as the National Union party, renominated Lincoln for President. Andrew Johnson, of Tennessee, was selected as candidate for Vice President. The Democrats of the North, assembled in Chicago, chose a general Lincoln had removed from command, George B. McClellan, as their candidate. In the election that November, Lincoln was re-elected easily, with a popular majority of over 400,000.

He thanked his friends and fellow-citizens, when they came to serenade him on the night of the election.

I am thankful to God for this approval of the people. But while deeply grateful for this mark of their confidence in me, if I know my heart, my gratitude is free from any taint of personal triumph. I do not impugn the motives of any one opposed to me. It is no pleasure for me to triumph over any one; but I give thanks to the Almighty for this evidence of the people's resolution to stand by free government and the rights of humanity.

The war was drawing to an end. Steadily the Union forces were advancing. William Tecumseh Sherman had taken Atlanta and Savannah. Charleston had fallen. Philip H. Sheridan was sweeping the Shenandoah Valley. There were peace overtures. Lincoln and Seward had conferred with Confederate Vice President Alexander H. Stephens and two southern peace commissioners. On Saturday, March 4, 1865, Lincoln once again appeared at the east portico of the Capitol. This time the oath was administered to the President by Chief Justice Salmon Portland Chase. Lincoln spoke to his fellow-countrymen and to all of humanity for all time.

At this second appearing to take the oath of the presidential office, there is less occasion for an extended address than there was at the first. Then a statement, somewhat in detail, of a course to be pursued, seemed fitting and proper. Now, at the expiration of four years, during which public declarations have been constantly called forth on every point and phase of the great contest which still absorbs the attention, and engrosses the energies of the nation, little that is new could be presented. The progress of our arms, upon which all else chiefly depends, is as well known to the public as to myself; and it is, I trust, reasonably satisfactory and encouraging to all. With high hopes for the future, no prediction in regard to it is ventured.

Neither party expected for the war, the magnitude, or the duration, which it has already attained. Neither anticipated that the *cause* of the conflict might cease with, or even before, the conflict itself should cease. Each looked for an easier triumph, and a result less fundamental and astounding. Both read the same Bible, and pray to the same God; and each invokes His aid against the other. It may seem strange that any men should dare to ask a just God's assistance in wringing their bread from the sweat of other men's faces; but let us judge not that we be not judged. The prayers of both could not be answered; that of neither has been answered fully. The Almighty has His own purposes. . . . Fondly do we hope—fervently do we pray—that this mighty scourge of war may speedily pass away. Yet, if God wills that it continue, until all the wealth piled by the bondman's two hundred and fifty years of unrequited toil shall be sunk, and until every drop of blood drawn with the lash, shall be paid by another drawn with the sword, as was said three thousand years ago, so still it must be said "the judgments of the Lord, are true and righteous altogether."

With malice toward none; with charity for all; with firmness in the right, as God gives us to see the right, let us strive on to finish the work we are in; to bind up the nation's wounds; to care for him who shall have borne the battle, and for his widow, and his orphan—to do all which may achieve and cherish a just, and a lasting peace, among ourselves, and with all nations.

Death, abstractly considered, is the same
with the high as with the low; but practically,
we are not so much aroused to the contemplation
of our own mortal natures, . . . as that of one
great and well known name.

FORD'S THEATRE

The armies of the South were retreating on all fronts. General
Sheridan had the Shenandoah Valley under control and now
had moved east to join Grant. Sherman was moving north
along the coast, pausing to inflict another defeat on the Confederates at Bentonville, North Carolina. Federal cavalry
under Major General James Harrison Wilson carried on raids
from Nashville to Selma and Montgomery. There was little
that Robert E. Lee could do to stave off the inevitable. On
April 1, Sheridan defeated the Confederates under George E.
Pickett at Five Forks. On April 3, the Davis government
abandoned Richmond, the Confederate capital. Lee and his
dwindling army moved west. The President sent a congratu-
latory telegram to Grant.

Allow me to tender you, and all with you, the nation's
grateful thanks for this additional and magnificent success. At your kind suggestion, I think I will visit you
tomorrow.

On April 4th Lincoln walked the streets of Richmond. Lee's army continued to try to elude the Union army. On April 9, Lee sent a flag of truce and asked for a meeting with Grant at Appomattox Court House. It was here that the Union general accepted the surrender of the Confederate Army of Northern Virginia. The fleeing Confederate government had moved to Greensboro, North Carolina, and was preparing to move to Charlotte. Back in Washington, the President responded to a serenade.

I am very greatly rejoiced to find that an occasion has occurred so pleasurable that the people cannot restrain themselves. . . . I see you have a band of music with you. . . . I have always thought "Dixie" one of the best tunes I have ever heard. Our adversaries over the way attempted to appropriate it, but I insisted yesterday that we fairly captured it. I presented this question to the Attorney General, and he gave it as his legal opinion that it is our lawful prize. I now request the band to favor me with its performance.

On the evening of Tuesday, April 11th, President Lincoln made his last public address. He spoke from a window to an immense crowd gathered at the White House. He had prepared his remarks in advance—he wanted to be certain that his remarks would not be misunderstood.

We meet this evening, not in sorrow, but in gladness of heart. The evacuation of Petersburg and Richmond, and the surrender of the principal insurgent army, give hope of a righteous and speedy peace whose joyous expression can not be restrained. In the midst of this, however, He, from Whom all blessings flow, must not be forgotten. A call for a national thanksgiving is being prepared, and will be duly promulgated. Nor must those whose harder part gives us the cause of rejoicing, be overlooked. Their honors must not be parcelled out with others. I myself, was near the front, and had the high pleasure of transmitting much of the good news to you; but no part of the honor, for plan or execution, is mine. To General Grant, his skillful officers, and brave men, all belongs. The gallant Navy stood ready, but was not in reach to take an active part.

By these recent successes the re-inauguration of the national authority—reconstruction—which has had a large share of thought from the first, is pressed more closely upon our attention. It is fraught with great difficulty. Unlike the case of a war between independent nations, there is no organized organ for us to treat with. No one man has authority to give up the rebellion for any other man. We simply must begin with, and mould from, disorganized and discordant elements. Nor is it a small additional embarrassment that we, the loyal people, differ among ourselves as to the mode, manner, and means of reconstruction.

Three nights later, in the company of Mrs. Lincoln, he attended a performance of a popular comedy by Tom Taylor, *Our American Cousin*, at Ford's Theatre, on Tenth Street, a few blocks east of the White House. At about ten o'clock, during the second scene of the third act, John Wilkes Booth, a member of the famous family of actors, entered the Presidential box. He quickly placed a small pistol close to the President's head, and fired a single shot. The Chief Executive slumped limply in his rocking chair, unconscious. He was carried across the street to a house owned by a tailor, William Petersen, and placed in a bed in a back room on the first floor. All through the night, Mrs. Lincoln, son Robert, cabinet members, surgeons and physicians kept their vigil. It was obvious to all that the wound was fatal. There was nothing they could do, except try to make him comfortable. He never regained consciousness.

At 7:22 on the morning of Saturday, April 15, 1865, Abraham Lincoln, Sixteenth President of the United States, breathed his last. He, too, had paid "the last full measure of devotion."

Let him have the marble monument, along with the well-assured and more enduring one in the hearts of those who love liberty, unselfishly, for all men.

THE MEMORIAL

The oracle of American democracy was dead; his spirit would live forever.

It would live on in his soaring Springfield tomb, and in the house at Eighth and Jackson; in the halls of the nearby State Capitol, and in New Salem by the banks of the Sangamon; where once he ran down the dim trails of old Kentucky on bare, boyish feet, or paced in cow-hide boots the rambling Indiana traces; where once he rode his slow rounds in the good days of the Illinois judicial circuit; where once again more slowly he walked the troubled ways of war-time Washington.

His spirit would glow out from the deeds and the words he wrote and spoke; whether at portico of Capitol or in the curving cemetery where slept the Gettysburg dead. His spirit would live on in the minds and homes of the world; but nowhere would it be felt more profoundly than in the vast and looming Memorial that had been ennobled by millions from everywhere.

But finally for all, the meek and the great, the powerful and the poor; the people—the common people he said God loved so much—for all of us, wherever we may be, whatever our station in life; he lives forever, for all generations, his spirit enshrined in our hearts.

A capacity, and a taste, for reading, gives access to whatever has already been discovered by others. It is the key, or one of the keys, to the already solved problems. . . . It gives a relish, and facility, for successfully pursuing the unsolved ones.

A LIBRARY OF ESSENTIAL LINCOLNIANA

In books, monographs, pamphlets, and other forms, more than ten thousand titles exist relating to Abraham Lincoln. This volume briefly relates his life story as he himself told it; and with characteristic simple eloquence and brevity, he did it superbly.

For those who would like to pursue the Lincoln story in more detail, the editor here presents a selected list chosen from the vast store of Lincoln literature. This selective bibliography has been divided into ten sections to make it easier for those who wish to make a deeper study.

The original edition of a title is listed along with any new edition containing significant additions to the text or useful editorial comment. If the work is still in print at the time of the publication of this volume, that is indicated by the symbol (p); if it has been reprinted in an offset or paperback edition, that fact is made known by the symbol (r).

I have tried to avoid listing works that are rare and difficult to obtain. Most of the out-of-print titles should be available in larger public libraries, college and historical libraries.

I. THE WORDS OF ABRAHAM LINCOLN

ANGLE, PAUL MCCLELLAND, and EARL SCHENCK MIERS, editors
*The Living Lincoln: The Man, His Mind, His Times, and
the War He Fought, Reconstructed from His Own Wrtings.*
New Brunswick: Rutgers University Press, 1955.
A skillfully edited single-volume edition of Lincoln's writ-
ings, based on *The Collected Works of Abraham Lincoln.*

BASLER, ROY PRENTICE, editor; MARION DOLORES PRATT and LLOYD
A. DUNLAP, assistant editors
The Collected Works of Abraham Lincoln. Nine (9)
volumes. New Brunswick: Rutgers University Press, 1953–
55. (p)
The definitive edition of the writings and speeches of Abraham Lincoln.

BASLER, ROY PRENTICE, editor
*The Collected Works of Abraham Lincoln: Supplement
1832–1865.* Westport: Greenwood Press, 1974. (p)
New writings of Lincoln discovered since the publication
of the previous work.

BASLER, ROY PRENTICE, editor
Abraham Lincoln: His Speeches and Writings. Preface by
Carl Sandburg. Cleveland and New York: The World
Publishing Company, 1946. (r)
The best of the single-volume collections of Lincoln's
works.

HERTZ, EMANUEL, editor
Lincoln Talks: A Bibliography in Anecdote. New York:
The Viking Press, 1939.
The most complete collection of Lincoln stories and humor.

KERNER, FRED, editor
A Treasury of Lincoln Quotations. Garden City: Doubleday
& Company, Inc., 1965.
An indispensable reference work for the best of the famous
as well as the little-known Lincoln quotations.

II. THE BIOGRAPHIES OF ABRAHAM LINCOLN

ANGLE, PAUL McCLELLAND, editor
The Lincoln Reader. New Brunswick: Rutgers University Press, 1947. New edition, Chicago: Rand McNally & Company, 1964.
From a century of reminiscences and writings about our sixteenth President the editor has assembled a full-length portrait as told by sixty-five different authors.

BEVERIDGE, ALBERT JEREMIAH
Abraham Lincoln, 1809–1858. Two (2) volumes. Boston and New York: Houghton Mifflin Company, 1928. (r)
A great lawyer and United States senator tells the story up to the time of the Lincoln-Douglas debates. Superb treatment of Lincoln as a lawyer and legislator.

HERNDON, WILLIAM HENRY, and JESSE WILLIAM WEIK
Herndon's Lincoln: The True Story of a Great Life. Three (3) volumes. Chicago: Belford, Clarke & Company, 1889. One-volume edition, with an Introduction and Notes by Paul M. Angle, Cleveland and New York: The World Publishing Company, 1949. Another one-volume edition, edited by David Freeman Hawke, Indianapolis: Bobbs-Merrill, 1970. (p)
The life of Lincoln as told by his law partner, with the assistance of Jesse W. Weik. With all of its personal prejudices, this is the great source work on the real man. All Lincoln biographers are indebted to Herndon for the material he unearthed and preserved.

NEWMAN, RALPH GEOFFREY, editor
Lincoln for the Ages. Forward by David C. Mearns. Garden City: Doubleday & Company, 1970. New edition, New York: Pyramid Books, 1964.
Seventy-six distinguished Americans including Bruce Catton, John Hope Franklin, Allan Nevins, Carl Sandburg and Adlai E. Stevenson each contribute a phase of the saga, resulting

in a most unusual and fresh biography of the Prairie President.

NICOLAY, JOHN GEORGE, and JOHN HAY

Abraham Lincoln: A History. Ten (10) volumes. New York: The Century Company, 1890. One-volume, abridged edition, edited by Paul M. Angle, Chicago: University of Chicago Press, 1966. (p)

Lincoln's two wartime secretaries collaborated in this indispensable source work. Much of the material is based on firsthand observation and knowledge. Not a fully objective work, it nevertheless must be included in any list of primary reference books about the Civil War President.

SANDBURG, CARL

Abraham Lincoln: The Prairie Years. The War Years. Six (6) volumes. New York: Harcourt, Brace & Company, 1926, 1939. (p). One-volume edition, New York: 1954. (p). One-volume, illustrated edition, New York: Harcourt Brace Jovanovich, 1970 (p)

A literary masterpiece. The longest of all Lincoln biographies, in which a great poet demonstrates that he can write magnificent history and biography.

TARBELL, IDA MINERVA

The Life of Abraham Lincoln. Two (2) volumes. New York: The Doubleday & McClure Co., 1900. Revised edition, New York: The Macmillan Company, 1928. (r)

One of the best of the early biographies. Tarbell interviewed many of the persons who knew Lincoln, and we are indebted to her for preserving many of their recollections.

THOMAS, BENJAMIN PLATT

Abraham Lincoln: A Biography. New York: Alfred A. Knopf, 1952. New edition, New York: The Modern Library, 1968. (p)

The best single-volume biography, and possibly the best of all Lincoln biographies. Well-written, sound in its historical judgments, it is a classic work.

III. THE LINCOLN FAMILY

GOFF, JOHN S.
Robert Todd Lincoln: A Man in His Own Right. Norman:
University of Oklahoma Press, 1969. (p)
The only full-length study of Abraham Lincoln's oldest
son, who became Secretary of War, U. S. Minister to
Great Britain, a prominent attorney, and a highly successful
corporation president.

LINCOLN, ROBERT TODD
*A Portrait of Abraham Lincoln in Letters by his Oldest
Son.* Edited by Paul M. Angle with the assistance of Richard
G. Case. Chicago: The Chicago Historical Society, 1969. (p)
A different viewpoint of Lincoln as gleaned from the
only published collection of letters written by his son.

RANDALL, RUTH PAINTER
Mary Lincoln: Biography of a Marriage. Boston: Little,
Brown and Company, 1953. (p)
A sympathetic biography of Mrs. Abraham Lincoln.

RANDALL, RUTH PAINTER
Lincoln's Sons. Boston: Little, Brown and Company,
1955. (p)
A study of the four Lincoln boys: Robert Todd, Edward
Baker, William Wallace, and Thomas ("Tad").

ROSS, ISHBEL
The President's Wife, Mary Todd Lincoln: A Biography.
New York: G. P. Putnam's Sons, 1973. (p)
An experienced and talented biographer presents a
perceptive in-depth portrait of a fascinating but much
misunderstood woman.

TURNER, JUSTIN G., and LINDA LEVITT TURNER
Mary Todd Lincoln: Her Life and Letters. With an
Introduction by Fawn M. Brodie. New York: Alfred A.
Knopf, 1972. (p)
All of the known letters of Mary Lincoln are here gathered

together and with the editors' skillful text present an unusual and intimate study of Mrs. Lincoln.

IV. THE PLACES IN LINCOLN'S LIFE

ANGLE, PAUL McCLELLAND
"Here I Have Lived." A History of Lincoln's Springfield, 1821–1865. Springfield: The Abraham Lincoln Association, 1935. Revised Edition, Chicago: Abraham Lincoln Book Shop, 1971. (p)
A carefully written, never dull, account of the community in which Lincoln rose from relative obscurity to the presidency.

BARINGER, WILLIAM ELDON
Lincoln's Vandalia: A Pioneer Portrait. New Brunswick: Rutgers University Press, 1949.
The story of Illinois' second capital, where Lincoln spent his first years in the legislature.

BROOKS, NOAH
Washington in Lincoln's Time. New York: The Century Company, 1895. New edition, edited with an Introduction by Herbert Mitgang, New York: Rinehart & Company, 1958.

HOLMES, FRED L.
Abraham Lincoln Traveled This Way. The Log Book of a Pilgrim in the Lincoln Country. Foreword by Glenn Frank. Boston: L. C. Page & Company, 1930.
A combination biography, guide and travel book.

MIERS, EARL SCHENCK, editor-in-chief
Lincoln Day by Day: A Chronology, 1809–1865. Compiled by William E. Baringer and based on the work of Paul M. Angle, Lloyd A. Dunlap, C. Percy Powell, Harry E. Pratt, and Benjamin P. Thomas. Three (3) volumes. Washington: Lincoln Sesquicentennial Commission, 1960.
An invaluable reference work. Records every known activity for Abraham Lincoln during his lifetime. Sets down where he was and what he did.

Tarbell, Ida Minerva
In the Footsteps of the Lincolns. New York: Harper &
Brothers, 1924.
The story of the places where Lincoln and his forebears
lived from Hingham, Massachusetts, to Springfield,
Illinois.

Thomas, Benjamin Platt
Lincoln's New Salem. Drawings by Romaine Proctor.
Springfield: The Abraham Lincoln Association, 1934. New
and Revised edition, with Introduction by Ralph G.
Newman, Chicago: Lincoln's New Salem Enterprises,
1973. (p)
This book covers the New Salem years of Abraham
Lincoln so thoroughly that no study of the subject can
be made without it. It is an American classic.

V. LINCOLN'S PARENTAGE AND YOUTH

Barton, William Eleazar
*The Paternity of Abraham Lincoln: Was He the Son of
Thomas Lincoln?* New York: George H. Doran Company.
1920.
A careful examination of the allegation that Abraham
Lincoln was an illegitimate child, resulting in a complete
refutation of the charge.

Barton, William Eleazar
The Lineage of Lincoln. Indianapolis: The Bobbs-Merrill
Company, 1929.
The history of the Lincoln and Hanks families.

Warren, Louis Austin
*Lincoln's Parentage and Childhood. A History of the
Kentucky Lincolns Supported by Documentary Evidence.*
New York: The Century Co., 1926.
The first thorough examination of Lincoln's Kentucky
years.

Warren, Louis Austin
Lincoln's Youth, Indiana Years, Seven to Twenty-one,

1816–1830. New York: Appleton-Century-Crofts, 1959.
The definitive work on this phase of Lincoln's life.

VI. THE FACE AND FEATURES OF ABRAHAM LINCOLN

BULLARD, FREDERICK LAURISTON
Lincoln, in Marble and Bronze. New Brunswick: Rutgers
University Press, 1952.
The story of sixty-eight heroic statues of Abraham Lincoln.
LORANT, STEFAN
Lincoln, His Life in Photographs. New York: Duell, Sloan
and Pearce, 1941. Revised and enlarged edition, *Lincoln:
A Picture Story of His Life.* New York: W. W. Norton
& Company, 1969. (p)
One of the great photographic editors of our time here
presents the Lincoln story in photographs.
MESERVE, FREDERICK HILL, and CARL SANDBURG
The Photographs of Abraham Lincoln. New York:
Harcourt, Brace and Company, 1947.
The first careful study of all of the known photographs.
With an essay on the subject by Carl Sandburg.
OSTENDORF, LLOYD, and CHARLES HAMILTON
Lincoln in Photographs. An Album of Every Known Pose.
Norman: University of Oklahoma Press, 1962. (p)
The most thorough study of Lincoln photographs.
Includes many new and exciting discoveries.

VII. ABRAHAM LINCOLN IN POLITICS

ANGLE, PAUL MCCLELLAND, editor
*Created Equal? The Complete Lincoln-Douglas Debates
of 1858.* Chicago: The University of Chicago Press,
1958. (p)
The complete text of the famous debates together with
the best account of this famous political duel.

Baringer, William Elsey

Lincoln's Rise to Power. Boston: Little, Brown and Company, 1937. (r)

The absorbing account of Lincoln's political progress from the delivery of his famous "House Divided" speech in 1858 until his election to the presidency in 1860.

Baringer, William Elsey

A House Dividing: Lincoln as President Elect. Springfield: The Abraham Lincoln Association, 1945.

A study of the four months between Lincoln's election in 1860 and his taking the oath of office on March 4, 1861.

Carman, Harry James, and Reinhard Henry Luthin

Lincoln and the Patronage. New York: Columbia University Press, 1943. (r)

How Lincoln handled the filling of the many federal offices which had been occupied by Democrats for several administrations.

Luthin, Reinhard Henry

The First Lincoln Campaign. Cambridge: Harvard University Press, 1944. (r)

An analysis of Lincoln's successful campaign for the presidency in 1860.

Nevins, Allan

The Ordeal of the Union. Eight (8) volumes. New York: Charles Scribner's Sons, 1947–71. (p)

A superb study of both the political and military history of the United States from 1847 to 1865, in which Abraham Lincoln's role is depicted in a masterful manner. The work is divided into three main sections: Volumes I and II, *The Ordeal of the Union, 1847–1857;* Volumes III and IV, *The Emergence of Lincoln, 1857–1861;* Volumes V, VI, VII and VIII, *The War for the Union, 1861–1865.*

Ordeal of the Union, Selected Chapters. Compiled and introduced by E. B. Long. New York: Charles Scribner's Sons, 1973. (p)

A one-volume condensation of the longer work.

Randall, James Garfield

Lincoln the President. Four (4) volumes. Volume IV edited and completed by Richard N. Current. New York: Dodd, Mead & Company, 1945–55. (r)
A great student of Lincoln's career presents a superb study of the presidential years.
Mr. Lincoln. Edited by Richard N. Current. New York: Dodd, Mead & Company, 1957. (r)
A single-volume distillation of *Lincoln the President.*
RIDDLE, DONALD WAYNE
Congressman Abraham Lincoln. Urbana: The University of Illinois Press, 1957.
The best account of Lincoln's single term in the United States Congress, 1847–49.
SIMON, PAUL
Lincoln's Preparation for Greatness: The Illinois Legislative Years. Norman: The University of Oklahoma Press, 1965. (r)
A former member of the Illinois House and Senate and lieutenant governor carefully studies Lincoln's period in the Legislature from 1834 to 1842.
WILLIAMS, T[HOMAS] HARRY
Lincoln and the Radicals. Madison: The University of Wisconsin Press, 1941. (r)
The author studies the bitter struggle between Lincoln and the radicals in his own party to control the conduct of the war.

VIII. LINCOLN AS COMMANDER-IN-CHIEF

BALLARD, COLIN ROBERT
The Military Genius of Abraham Lincoln. London: Oxford University Press, 1926. New edition, with a Preface by Fletcher Pratt, Cleveland and New York: The World Publishing Company, 1952.
Brigadier General Ballard, an English soldier, studies Lincoln's role as a wartime leader from the viewpoint of the professional soldier.

BRUCE, ROBERT VANCE

Lincoln and the Tools of War. Foreword by Benjamin P. Thomas. Indianapolis: The Bobbs-Merrill Company, 1956. (r)

An account of the arming of the Union forces in the Civil War and Lincoln's part in it.

WILLIAMS, T[HOMAS] HARRY

Lincoln and His Generals. New York: Alfred A. Knopf, 1952.

The author's theme is Lincoln as a director of war, his place in the high command, and his influence in developing a modern command system for this nation.

IX. SPECIAL STUDIES ABOUT ABRAHAM LINCOLN

CURRENT, RICHARD NELSON

The Lincoln Nobody Knows. New York: McGraw-Hill Book Company, 1958.

Dr. Current studies the man and the myth and the conflicts, paradoxes, and seeming contradictions that surround Lincoln's life.

DONALD, DAVID

Lincoln's Herndon. Introduction by Carl Sandburg. New York: Alfred A. Knopf, 1948.

The definitive biography of Lincoln's law partner, William Henry Herndon.

DUFF, JOHN JOSEPH

A. Lincoln, Prairie Lawyer. New York: Rinehart & Company, 1960.

A thorough and carefully researched account of Lincoln as a lawyer from 1837 to 1861.

HARPER, ROBERT STORY

Lincoln and the Press. New York: McGraw-Hill Book Company, 1951.

The newspaper story of Lincoln from the day in 1836 when his name first appeared in print to the time of his death in 1865.

MITGANG, HERBERT, editor
Lincoln: As They Saw Him. New York: Rinehart &
Company, 1956. New edition, *Abraham Lincoln: A Press
Portrait*, Chicago and New York: Quadrangle Books,
1971. (p)
A contemporaneous picture of Lincoln compiled entirely
from original sources.
MONAGHAN, [JAMES] JAY
Lincoln Bibliography, 1839–1939. Two (2) volumes.
Foreword by James G. Randall. Springfield: Illinois State
Historical Library, 1943, 1945.
The most complete listing of Lincoln literature, though
it was published thirty-five years ago and does not include
the many excellent titles issued since 1939.
MONAGHAN, [JAMES] JAY
*Diplomat in Carpet Slippers: Abraham Lincoln Deals with
Foreign Affairs.* Indianapolis: The Bobbs-Merrill Company,
1945. (r)
A lively account of foreign policy and problems under
President Lincoln.
PRATT, HARRY EDWARD
The Personal Finances of Abraham Lincoln. Springfield:
The Abraham Lincoln Association, 1943.
Refutes the myth of the impecunious young lawyer and
reveals Lincoln as a successful lawyer, who left an estate
that amounted to more than $100,000 by the time it was
distributed.
THOMAS, BENJAMIN PLATT
Portrait for Posterity: Lincoln and His Biographers. New
Brunswick: Rutgers University Press, 1947. (r)
Every important Lincoln biographer (up to 1947) is
discussed with charm and perception.
WILSON, RUFUS ROCKWELL, editor
Intimate Memories of Abraham Lincoln. Elmira: The
Primavera Press, 1945.
More than eighty persons who knew Lincoln recall him.
Each contributor is identified, and the circumstances of the
first appearance of the reminiscence are indicated.

X. THE DEATH AND FUNERAL OF ABRAHAM LINCOLN

BRYAN, CHARLES SANDS
The Great American Myth. New York: Carrick & Evans, 1940.
A careful examination of the evidence in the Lincoln assassination and a refutation of many of the myths which have persisted for a century.

EISENSCHIML, OTTO
Why Was Lincoln Murdered? Boston: Little, Brown and Company, 1937. New edition, New York: Grosset & Dunlap, 1957.
An exciting, though controversial, view of the death of Abraham Lincoln. The author's painstaking research reveals some new facts about the crime.

KUNHARDT, DOROTHY MESERVE, and PHILIP B. KUNHARDT
Twenty Days: A Narrative in Text and Pictures of the Assassination of Abraham Lincoln and the Twenty Days and Nights That Followed . . . Foreword by Bruce Catton. New York: Harper & Row, 1965.
The best account of the incredible funeral with excellent illustrations, some never published before.

LEWIS, LLOYD DOWNS
Myths After Lincoln. New York: Harcourt, Brace and Company, 1929. New edition, with an Introduction by Carl Sandburg, New York: Harcourt, Brace and Company, 1940. (r)
One of the most fascinating and best-written books about Lincoln. Is mainly devoted to Lincoln's death and the myths that followed. The description of the funeral as "Half Circus, Half Heartbreak" is one of the classics in Lincolniana.

ROSCOE, THEODORE
The Web of Conspiracy: The Complete Story of the Men Who Murdered Abraham Lincoln. Englewood Cliffs: Prentice-Hall, 1959.

The most careful and thorough collection of material relating to the Lincoln assassination. It is difficult to contemplate any research on this phase of the Lincoln story which would improve on this work.

*It is found in nearly all the published
speeches of him who now addresses you. I
do but quote from one of those speeches . . .*

REFERENCE SOURCES FOR
QUOTATIONS USED AS
CHAPTER HEADINGS

TITLE PAGE: Copybook verses (1824–26); page 1.
From a self-made arithmetic book made by Abraham Lincoln as a boy in Indiana. His stepmother, Sarah Bush Johnston Lincoln, gave the volume to William H. Herndon, who
was Lincoln's law partner from 1844 to 1861. Herndon
took the book apart and dispersed the pages. Ten leaves
have been located and all are reproduced in *The Collected
Works of Abraham Lincoln,* Volume I, pages xxvii–xxix,
Rutgers University Press, New Brunswick, New Jersey
(1953–55).

FOREWORD: Letter to Samuel Galloway; June 19, 1860.
The Collected Works of Abraham Lincoln, Volume IV,
page 80.

KENTUCKY BIRTH: Fragment of speech intended for Kentuckians;
ca. February 12, 1861.
The Collected Works of Abraham Lincoln, Volume IV,
page 200.

INDIANA YEARS: Remarks at Indiana state line; February 11, 1861.
The Collected Works of Abraham Lincoln, Volume IV,
page 192.

SISTER SARAH: Letter to Samuel Haycraft; May 28, 1860.
The Collected Works of Abraham Lincoln, Volume IV,
page 56.

TRIP TO NEW ORLEANS: Letter to Nathaniel P. Banks; August 5,
1863.
The Collected Works of Abraham Lincoln, Volume VI,
page 364.

MOVE TO ILLINOIS: Letter to John A. McClernand; November
10, 1861.
The Collected Works of Abraham Lincoln, Volume V,
page 20.

BLACK HAWK WAR: Letter to Jesse W. Fell, enclosing autobi-
ography. December 20, 1859.
The Collected Works of Abraham Lincoln, Volume III,
page 512.

POSTMASTER AND SURVEYOR: Letter to John D. Johnston; November 4, 1851.
The Collected Works of Abraham Lincoln, Volume II,
page 111.

ILLINOIS LEGISLATOR: Letter to Owen Lovejoy; August 11, 1855.
The Collected Works of Abraham Lincoln, Volume II,
page 317.

SPRINGFIELD LAWYER: Fragment: notes for a law lecture; July 1,
1850?
The Collected Works of Abraham Lincoln, Volume II,
page 81.

MARRIAGE TO MARY TODD: Letter to Mary S. Owens; May 7,
1837.
The Collected Works of Abraham Lincoln, Volume I, page
78.

THE LINCOLN FAMILY: Letter to Jesse Lincoln; April 1, 1854. The
Lincolns had four sons. Edward Baker Lincoln, their second
child who was born in 1846, died in February 1850.
The Collected Works of Abraham Lincoln, Volume II, page
217.

UNITED STATES CONGRESSMAN: Letter to Joshua F. Speed; October
22, 1846.

The Collected Works of Abraham Lincoln, Volume I, page 391.

THE HOUSE DIVIDED: Speech at Springfield, Illinois; June 16, 1858.
The Collected Works of Abraham Lincoln, Volume II, page 461.

DEBATES WITH DOUGLAS: Speech at Chicago, Illinois; July 10, 1858.
The Collected Works of Abraham Lincoln, Volume II, page 488.

NOMINATION FOR PRESIDENT: Letter to James F. Babcock; April 14, 1860.
The Collected Works of Abraham Lincoln, Volume IV, page 43.

PRESIDENTIAL ELECTION: Speech from the steps of the capitol at Columbus, Ohio; February 13, 1861.
The Collected Works of Abraham Lincoln, Volume IV, page 205.

FAREWELL TO SPRINGFIELD: Remarks at Tolono, Illinois; February 11, 1861.
The Collected Works of Abraham Lincoln, Volume IV, page 191.

FIRST INAUGURAL: First Inaugural Address; March 4, 1861.
The Collected Works of Abraham Lincoln, Volume IV.

EMANCIPATION PROCLAMATION: Emancipation Proclamation; January 1, 1863.
The Collected Works of Abraham Lincoln, Volume VI, page 30.

COMMANDER-IN-CHIEF: Letter to Thomas H. Clay; October 8, 1862.
The Collected Works of Abraham Lincoln, Volume V, page 452.

GETTYSBURG ADDRESS: Letter to Salmon Portland Chase; November 17, 1863.
The Collected Works of Abraham Lincoln, Volume VII, page 15.

SECOND INAUGURAL: Reply to Notification Committee; March 1, 1865.

The Collected Works of Abraham Lincoln, Volume VIII, page 326.

FORD'S THEATRE: Eulogy on Zachary Taylor, Chicago, Illinois; July 25, 1850.

The Collected Works of Abraham Lincoln, Volume II, page 90.

THE MEMORIAL: Letter to John H. Byrant; May 30, 1864.

The Collected Works of Abraham Lincoln, Volume VII, page 366.

A LIBRARY OF ESSENTIAL LINCOLNIANA: Address before the Wisconsin State Agricultural Society, Milwaukee, Wisconsin; September 30, 1859.

The Collected Works of Abraham Lincoln, Volume III, pages 480–81.

REFERENCE SOURCES FOR QUOTATIONS USED AS CHAPTER HEADINGS: First Inaugural Address; March 4, 1861.

The Collected Works of Abraham Lincoln, Volume IV, pages 262–63.

INDEX: Address Before the Young Men's Lyceum of Springfield, Illinois; January 27, 1838.

The Collected Works of Abraham Lincoln, Volume I, page 113.

But the game is caught; and I believe it is true, that with the catching, end the pleasures of the chase. This field of glory is harvested. . . .

INDEX

A.B.C. schools, 9, 12
Alabama, secession of, 59, 65
Antietam Creek, battle at, 69
Appomattox Court House, 90
Arkansas, secession of, 65
Army of the Potomac, 73, 77
Ashmun, George, 53
Ashmun Amendment, 39

Baker, Edward D., 41
Bates, Edward, 53
Bell, John, 56, 57
Berry, William F., 29
Black Hawk (Indian chief),
  25–26
Black Hawk War, 25, 26
Boat building, 21
Booth, John Wilkes, 91
Breckinridge, John C., 55, 56, 57
Brumfield, William and Nancy
  Lincoln, 8
Buchanan, James, 45
Bull Run, second battle of, 69
Burnside, Ambrose E., 67, 73, 74

Cameron, Simon, 53

Cass, Lewis, 26
Chancellorsville, battle of, 77
Chase, Salmon Portland, 53, 86
Chester County (Pa.) *Times*, 3
Chicago Press and Tribune, 3
"Chronicles of Reuben, The"
  (Lincoln), 16
Civil War, 64–65, 67–68, 73–75,
  77–81, 83, 84, 85
Clay, Henry, 26, 32
Confederate Army, 64, 69, 77, 78,
  89, 90
Confederate States of America,
  59, 89
Constitutional Union Party, 56
Cooper Institute, 51
Crawford, Andrew, 13
Crume, Ralph and Mary Lincoln,
  8

Davis, David, 53
Davis, Jefferson, 59, 89
Declaration of Independence, 61
Democratic party, 47, 55
  Northern, 56, 85
  Southern, 56

District of Columbia, 40
Dorsey, Azel W., 13
Douglas, Stephen A., 43, 55, 56, 57
 debates with Lincoln, 47–49
Draft riots, 83
Dred Scott decision, 44
Dresser, Charles, 35

Early, Jacob M., 25
Edwards, Ninian W. and Elizabeth Todd, 35
Emancipation Proclamation, 69–70
Everett, Edward, 56, 78, 79, 80
Ewing, W. L. W., 20

Fell, Jesse W., 3
"Fifty-four, forty, or fight," 40
Florida, secession of, 59, 65
Ford's Theatre, 91
Fort Sumter, 64, 65
Fox Indians, 25
Fremont, John C., 45

Gentry, Allen, 17
Gentry, James, 17
Georgia, secession of, 59, 65
Gettysburg, battle of, 78
Gettysburg address, 79–80
Grant, Ulysses S., 68, 74–75, 89, 90, 91
Great Britain, 37, 40
Greeley, Horace, 3
Grigsby, Aaron, 15–16
Grigsby, Charles, 16, 19
Grigsby, Reuben, 16
Grigsby, Sarah Lincoln (Mrs. Aaron Grigsby, sister of the President), 8–9, 15

Hamlin, Hannibal, 53
Hanks, Dennis, 9
Hanks, John, 19, 20, 21, 22–23, 52

Hanks, Nancy. See Lincoln, Nancy Hanks
Hardin, John J., 41
Harrison, William Henry, 32
Hazel, Caleb, 9
Herndon, Rowan, 29
Herndon, William H., 27, 34
Hill, Samuel, 27
Hooker, Joseph, 67, 73–74, 77, 78
Hunting, 11

Ile, Elijah, 25
Illinois
 Hanks family in, 8
 Thomas Lincoln family move to, 19–20
Illinois Journal, 44
Illinois Seventh (Congressional) District, 40
Illinois State Journal, 31
Illinois State Legislature, 31–32
Illinois State Republican Convention, 52
Indiana, Lincoln family in, 8, 11–12, 16

Jackson, Andrew, 26
Jackson, Thomas J. ("Stonewall"), 77
Johnson, Andrew, 85
Johnson, Herschel V., 56
Johnston, John D., 20, 21, 38
Johnston, Sally. See Lincoln, Sally
Judd, Norman B., 53

Kansas-Nebraska bill, 43
Kentucky
 in Civil War, 65
 Lincoln family in, 7–8

Lane, Joseph, 56
Lawyer, 31, 33–34, 43

Lee, Robert E., 69, 77, 78, 89, 90
Lewis, Joseph J., 3
Life of Abraham Lincoln (Scripps), 3
Lincoln, Abraham
    ancestors of, 7–9
    on his appearance, 49
    autobiographical sketches, 3–4
    boat building by, 21
    and Civil War. *See* Civil War
    death of, 91–92
    on the Declaration of Independence, 61
    on the Dred Scott decision, 44
    education, 9, 12–13
    Emancipation Proclamation, 69–70
    fence building by, 20
    as lawyer, 31, 33–34, 43
    marriage, 35–36
    memorable addresses by. *See* Memorable addresses
    Memorial, 93
    on the Mexican War, 39–40
    opponents in his Cabinet, 67
    poetry by, 15, 16
    political career. *See* Political career
    as postmaster, 29
    proclamation after Fort Sumter firing, 64–65
    on slavery, 32, 40, 60
    sons of, 37
    as storekeeper, 29–30
    as surveyor, 30, 31
    on the Union, 63–64, 84
Lincoln, Abraham (grandfather of the President), 7–8
    brothers of: Isaac, Jacob, John, and Thomas, 7
    sons of: Josiah and Mordecai, 8; Thomas (father of the President), *see below*
Lincoln, Edward Baker (son of the President), 37

Lincoln, Mary Ann Todd (Mrs. Abraham Lincoln), 35, 37–38, 91
Lincoln, Nancy Hanks (Mrs. Thomas Lincoln, mother of the President), 8, 12
Lincoln, Robert Todd (son of the President), 37, 91
Lincoln, Sally (Mrs. Thomas Lincoln, stepmother of the President), 12, 38
Lincoln, Sarah. *See* Grigsby, Sarah Lincoln
Lincoln, Thomas (brother of the President, died in infancy), 9
Lincoln, Thomas (father of the President), 8, 9, 12, 38
Lincoln, Thomas "Tad" (son of the President), 37
Lincoln, William Wallace (son of the President), 37
Lincoln-Douglas debates, 47–49
Lincolniana, 93
Logan, Stephen T., 34
"Lost Speech," 44
Louisiana, secession of, 59, 65

McClellan, George B., 67, 85
McNamar (McNeil), John, 27
Maryland, in Civil War, 65
Meade, George G., 68, 78
Memorable addresses
    at Cooper Institute, 51
    debates with Stephen A. Douglas, 47–49
    first inaugural address, 63–64
    first political speech, 20
    Gettysburg address, 79–80
    last public address, 90–91
    "Lost Speech," 44
    second inaugural address, 86–87
Mexican War, 39–40
Mississippi, secession of, 59, 65

Missouri, in Civil War, 65
Missouri Compromise, 43, 44

National Union party, 85
New Orleans trips, 17, 21–23
New Salem, Ill., 22, 25, 29–30
    state legislature candidate
    (defeated), 26–27
New York City, draft riots in,
    83
New York Tribune, 3

Offutt, Denton, 20–23, 25
Onstot, Henry, 22
Oregon boundary question, 40
Our American Cousin (play), 91
Owens, Mary, 27

Petersen, William, 91
Pickett, George E., 89
Poetry, 15, 16
Political career
    campaigning for John C.
        Fremont, 45
    canvassing for William Henry
        Harrison and Henry Clay,
        32
    canvassing for Zachary Taylor,
        41
    defeated for Illinois State
        Legislature, 26–27
    defeated for U. S. Senate, 44,
        49
    first political document signing,
        20
    first political speech, 20
    in Illinois State Legislature,
        31–32
    presidential elections, 51–54,
        55–57, 63–64, 85, 86–87
    as "rail splitter" candidate, 52
    as a Republican, 44, 45, 53, 85
    in U. S. House of
        Representatives, 39–41
    as a Whig, 32, 39, 43, 45
Pope, John, 67, 69

Posey, John F., 20
Postmaster, New Salem, Ill., 29
Pullman Company, 37

Rail fence building, 20
"Rail splitter" candidate, 52
Republican National Convention
    Chicago, 53
    Philadelphia, 45
Republican party, 85
    organization of, 44
Riney, Zachariah, 9
Rule of Three, 12
Rutledge, Ann, 27
Rutledge, James, 27

Sac Indians, 25
Scott, Winfield, 67
Scripps, John Locke, 3
Secession, 59, 65
Seward, William H., 53, 69, 85
Sheridan, Philip H., 85, 89
Sherman, William Tecumseh, 85,
    89
Slavery, 17, 31–32, 40, 43, 47, 48,
    49, 60
    Emancipation Proclamation,
        69–70
South Carolina, secession of, 59,
    65
Speed, Joshua Fry, 33, 35
Springfield, Ill., 33, 44, 93
    departure from, 60
Stephens, Alexander H., 59, 85
Stevenson, Adlai E., 3
Stone, Dan, 31
Storekeeper, 29–30
Stuart, John T., 31, 33, 34
Surveying, 30, 31
Swaney, James, 13

Taney, Roger B., 63
Taylor, Tom, 91
Taylor, Zachary, 39–40, 41
Tennessee, secession of, 65

Texas
    and Mexican War, 40
    secession of, 59, 65
Todd, Mary Ann. *See* Lincoln,
    Mary Ann Todd
Todd, Robert Smith, 35
Tribune Tracts No. 6, 3
Trumbull, Lyman, 44, 51

Union, the
    Lincoln on, 63–64, 84
    states seceding from, 59, 65
Union Army, 65, 69, 74, 77, 78,
    83, 85, 90

Vicksburg, campaign of, 74
Virginia
    Lincoln family in, 7–8
    secession of, 65

Weekly North-Western Gazette,
    44
Whig party, 32, 39, 43, 45
Wilson, James Harrison, 89

Yates, Richard, 43
Young Men's Republican Union,
    51